D1179111

GREENWICH & BLACKHEATH PAST

Greenwich in about 1856. The oldest known photograph from Observatory Hill shows the Queen's House, Royal Naval College and the Isle of Dogs, with sailing ships and masthouse in the misty distance.

Opposite:
Commuting to Greenwich in 1843.
(see p89)

GREENWICH AND BLACKHEATH PAST

by

Felix Barker

With additional material by
Denise Silvester-Carr

First Published 1993
Revised edition 1999
By Historical Publications Ltd
32 Ellington Street, London N7 8PL
(Tel: 0171-607 1628)

ISBN 0 948667 55 9

Typeset by Historical Publications Ltd
Reproduction by G & J Graphics, London EC2
Printed by Butler and Tanner, Frome, Somerset

The Illustrations

Sources of illustrations: public archives, private collections, institutions, photographers and books. Thanks are offered for kind permissions to publish and it is hoped there are no misleading attributions.

Greenwich Local History Library: 1, 2, 3, 4, 9, 10, 28, 38, 40, 43, 47, 50, 51, 52, 53, 55, 59, 60, 61, 62, 63, 64, 69, 71, 73, 97, 98, 99, 104, 105, 106, 110, 111, 115, 117, 118, 119, 121, 122, 124, 125, 126, 127, 128, 13, 131, 133, 134, 135, 136, 137, 143, 144, 147, 151, 153, 155, 162, 163, 165, 169, 170, 174, 176, 178, 179, 180, 181, 184, 185, 186, 189, 190, 192, 196, 199, 200, 201, 202, 203, 205, 208, 209, 211, 212
Lewisham Local History Library (covering Blackheath): 56, 70, 74, 86, 87, 88, 89, 93, 94, 138, 140, 141, 142, 150, 156, 157, 159, 167, 168, 171, 172
National Maritime Museum: 25, 27, 34, 39, 57, 85, 109, 221
Museum in Docklands: PLA Collection: frontispiece, 187, 188, 191, 193
Peter Jackson Collection: 1, 6, 14, 17, 19, 22, 26, 29, 31, 33, 36, 42, 44, 45, 49, 66, 81, 95, 114, 123, 129, 145, 149, 206
Author's Collection: title-page, 7, 8, 15, 30, 37, 41, 54, 65, 67, 72, 83, 84, 91, 100, 107, 112, 113, 116, 120, 126, 132, 139, 146, 148, 166, 177, 182, 183, 195, 197, 204, 210, 213, 216
Age Exchange, Blackheath: 173, 198; *Aerofilms Ltd*: 18; *Architectural Review*: 23; *Courtauld Institute of Art (Private collection)*: 32; *Eric Lyons Cunningham Partnership*: 214, 215; *London Topographical Society*: 175, 194; *New Millennium Experience Co*: 219; *Neil Rhind*: 75, 92, 152, 158, 160, 164; *Royal Collection Enterprises © 1993 Her Majesty the Queen*: 24; *Royal Commission on Historical Monuments for England*: 5; *Royal Institute of British Architects*: 101, 102, 103; *Denise Silvester-Carr*: 96, 217, 218, 220; *Worcester College, Oxford*: 21

Other illustrations come from the collections of *Roger Cline* or *Historical Publications Ltd.*

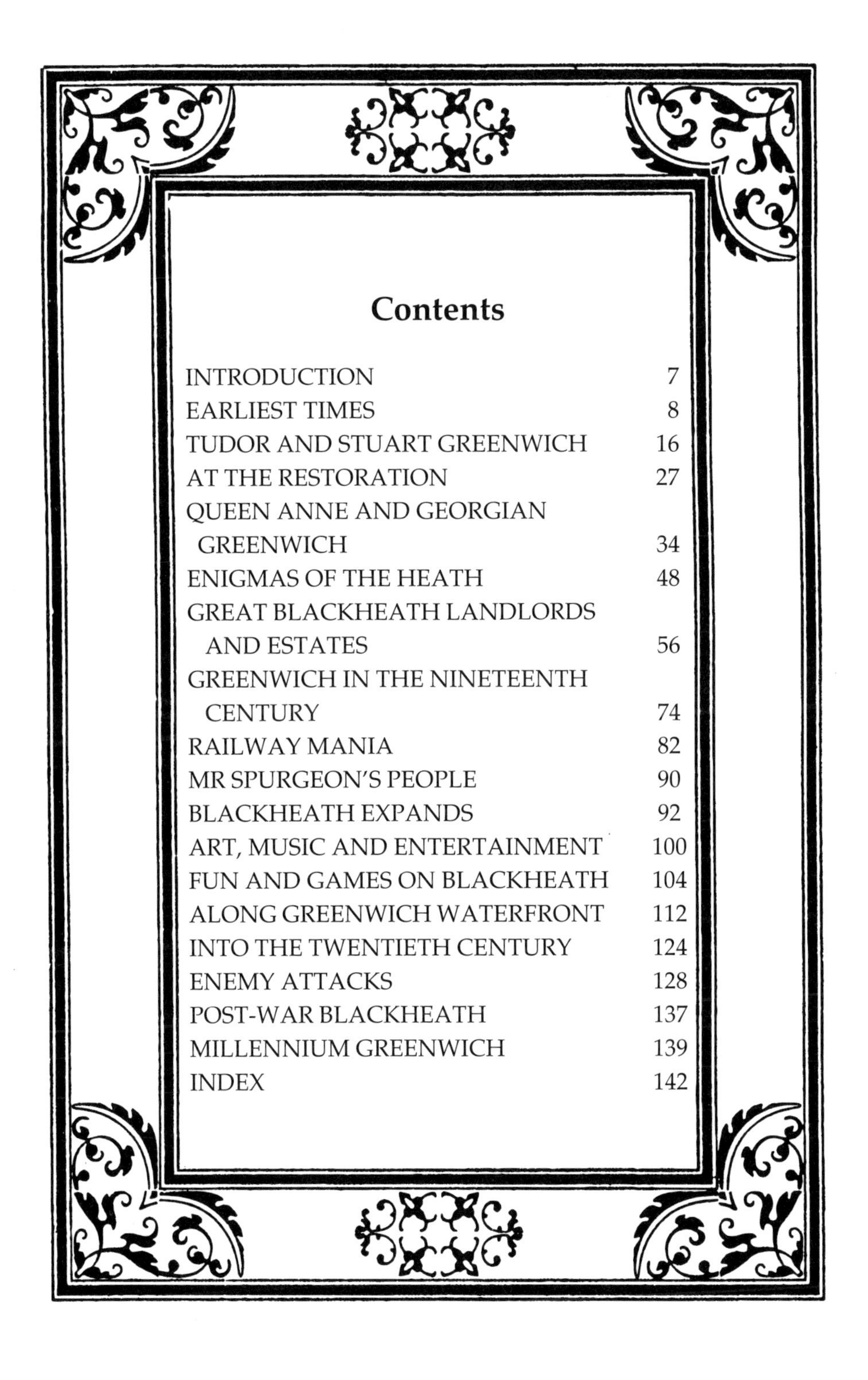

Contents

Acknowledgements

It is difficult to put down your foot anywhere in Blackheath without trespassing on ground which thanks to years of exploration Neil Rhind has made his own. His consultation of archives and burrowing into rate books has saved me endless basic research. I am greatly indebted to his three volumes of Blackheath history (see below) and keenly await one to come.

Greenwich, unfortunately, has not received such comprehensive investigation. Beryl Platts has written a history wonderfully detailed and evocative up to the end of the eighteenth century, but has not attempted to treat modern times so fully. *Transactions of the Greenwich and Lewisham Antiquarian Society* (with a general index up to 1981) fill in some gaps. A social, industrial and political history of Greenwich for the last two centuries is badly needed.

I am especially grateful to Julian Watson, head of Greenwich Local History Library, for his help and for making so many illustrations available. He expertly steered me through the tricky problems of Domesday, Hundreds and early Manors. John Coulter of Lewisham Local History Library (which covers Blackheath) has also been very helpful.

Peter Jackson has contributed generously, as he always does, in providing pictures from his incomparable London Collection. He has also made it possible to visualise the Tudor Palace of Greenwich by providing the plan which he has imposed on a modern aerial view. In addition he kindly helped with the sketch plan (p77) showing nineteenth-century street developments in Greenwich.

For innumerable details of research, correcting proofs and easing publication by putting my text onto a word processor I owe special thanks to Denise Silvester-Carr who has a sixth sense in detecting historical slips. My wife's encouragement as well as her proof-reading and painstaking checking of a long index has been of great help.

The mastermind behind Historical Publications would probably prefer to remain anonymous, but I think London should know of the dedicated enthusiasm and expertise of John Richardson who has made this and so many local histories possible.

F.B.

Further Reading

BAKER, Gerald L., *Blackheath, the Story of the Royal Hundred.* (Morden Society, 1925)

BONWITT, W., *The History of the Paragon.* (The Bookshop, Blackheath Ltd., undated)

BRYANT, Julius (Ed.), *Finest Prospects, Three Historic Houses (including Ranger's House)*; illustrated catalogue of thirty-four Blackheath and Greenwich views. (English Heritage, 1986)

CLARK, K.D., *Greenwich and Woolwich in Old Photographs.* (Alan Sutton 1990)

COULTER, John, *Lewisham and Deptford in Old Photographs.* (Alan Sutton, 1990)

COULTER, John, *Lewisham and Deptford in Old Photographs - a second selection.* (Alan Sutton, 1992) Both of these books by John Coulter cover Blackheath.

DIXON, Philip, *Excavations at Greenwich Palace 1970-1971.* (Greenwich and Lewisham Antiquarian Society, 1972)

GLENCROSS, Alan, *Grandfather's Greenwich.* From the Spurgeon Collection. (Conway Maritime Press, 1972)

HAMILTON, Olive and Nigel, *Royal Greenwich.* (Greenwich Bookshop, 1969)

HASTED, Edward, *History of Kent, Vol. I: The Hundred of Blackheath.* (1778)

HOWSE, Derek, *Greenwich Time.* (Oxford University Press, 1986)

JENKINS, Simon, *Outer London, Companion Guide to,* (Collins, 1981)

LAMBARDE, William, *Perambulation of Kent.* (1570)

NEWELL, Philip, *Greenwich Hospital, A Royal Foundation 1692-1983.* (Trustees of Greenwich Hospital, 1984)

PLATTS, Beryl, *A History of Greenwich.* (David and Charles, 1973)

RHIND, Neil, *Vol. I. Blackheath Village and Environs 1790-1970.* (1976)

Vol I., Wricklemarsh and the Cator Estate. (1983)

The Heath. (1987) All published by The Bookshop, Blackheath.

Vol III (in preparation) *Blackheath in Lee, from Lloyd's Place to Dartmouth Row; from The Point to Crooms Hill.*

SPURGEON, Darrell, *Discover Greenwich and Charlton.* (Greenwich Guidebooks, 1991)

STARKEY, David (Ed.), *Henry VIII, A European Court in England.* Catalogue of exhibition at National Maritime Museum. (Collins and Brown in association with the National Maritime Museum, 1991)

WATSON, Julian and GREGORY, Kit, *In the Meantime, a book on Greenwich* (Photographs of 19th-century demolitions). London Borough of Greenwich Tourism Section, 1988)

Introduction

Greenwich and Blackheath sit together as compatibly as twins four miles south-east of London Bridge, the town dangling its feet in the water, the village with its head in the air. They are complementary and in places overlap, but they are far from identical twins.

Greenwich is a workaday town with a waterfront that is largely industrial; Blackheath is a comfortable village on the edge of an open expanse where games are played, kites flown, dogs walked and fairs enjoyed. In compensation for Blackheath's rural charm, Greenwich can boast a long history, royal associations, spectacular views and monumental buildings that annually attract two million visitors.

Young Greenwich residents mostly working in London have made their homes in small houses that have more than a vestige of Regency charm. Blackheath also has a new generation of Span dwellers but people living in larger houses surrounding the Heath tend to be older and longer settled.

There is a forgivable vagueness about demarcation, and people whose houses share mutual fringes are apt to temporize when asked where they live. They may well say, 'Oh, in Greenwich – but up on the Heath' or else, 'We're in Blackheath – over on the Greenwich side.' They want the best of both worlds.

I first found myself experiencing this topographical confusion when we moved as a family to Blackheath – or so we thought – in 1957. A flat in Spencer Perceval House, Dartmouth Row, our home for three years, was historically in the Hundred of Blackheath; Domesday said so. But a 1695 Survey preferred us to be in the Manor of Greenwich. We then found that an Act of 1899 had delivered us into the borough of Lewisham while in 1917 the Post Office decided that our address was Greenwich.

We never really sorted it out before we moved across the Heath in 1960 to Lloyd's Place. As this was on the edge of the village, now we must surely be in Blackheath. Not at all; we were held in fee to Lewisham and were in North Lewisham when it came to voting.

These ambiguities have done nothing to diminish the pleasure I derive from the view my study in Lindsey House affords of the Heath with Greenwich in the distance. For thirty or more years it has been like overlooking a private park. I hope this book will be accepted as a mark of gratitude for enjoyment of a delightful environment.

FELIX BARKER
Lindsey House, Blackheath

MCMXCIII

Felix Barker died on 11 July 1997. He had been collecting material for this revised edition for some time. The chapter Post-War Blackheath has been revised, and the final chapter, Millennium Greenwich, has been written by Denise Silvester-Carr.

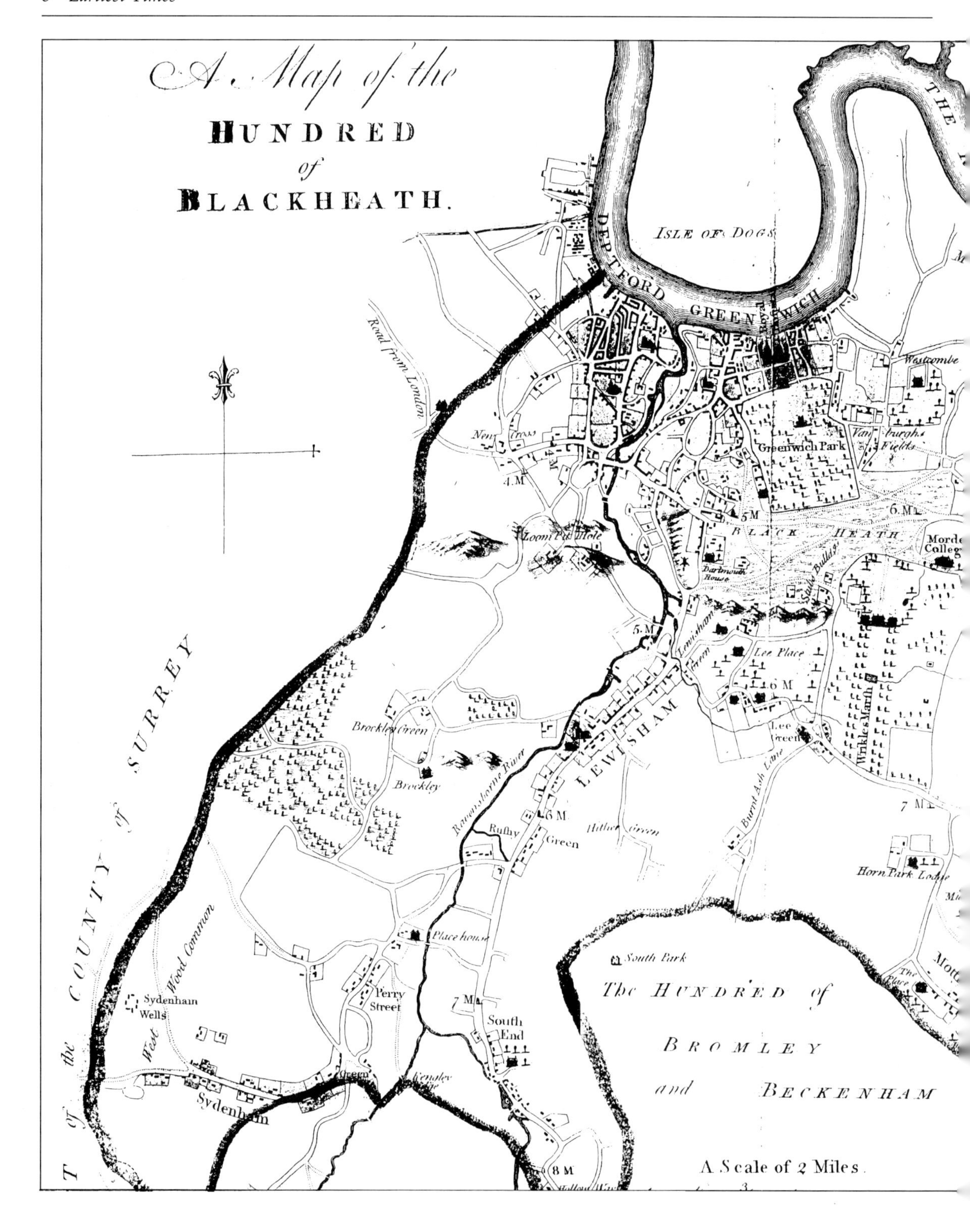
A Map of the
HUNDRED
of
BLACKHEATH.
ISLE OF DOGS
DEPTFORD
GREENWICH
Road from London
New Cross
Greenwich Park
Westcombe
Blackheath
Dartmouth House
Lee Place
Lee Green
Wrikles Marsh
Burnt Ash Lane
LEWISHAM
Brockley Green
Brockley
Ravensborne River
Rushy Green
Hither Green
Horn Park Lodge
Place house
The County of Surrey
West Wood Common
Sydenham Wells
Sydenham
Perry Street
South End
South Park
The Hundred of Bromley and Beckenham
A Scale of 2 Miles

Earliest Times

GREEN PORT AND BLEAK HEATH

The derivation of the names Greenwich and Blackheath remain uncertain. Place-name scholars agree that Greenwich means 'the Green Port' (a place where gravel or sand came down to the river's edge to make landings possible). William Lambarde, the Elizabethan historian who had a house on the north side of the Heath, believed that the name Blackheath came from the 'colour of the soile', but it is more probably a corruption of 'Bleak' heath. The basic Anglo-Saxon words 'Black' and 'Heath' do not provide precise interpretation.

Both places are very old indeed; they antedate Alfred the Great, but there is no archaeological evidence to support a once-held theory that there was a Celtic, pre-Roman settlement on the north-west part of the Heath. This means a parallel deduction – that Crooms Hill ('twisting hill') is London's oldest thoroughfare used by prehistoric people – is attractive but fanciful.

The map from Edward Hasted's eighteenth-century *History of Kent*, left, is dotted with familiar names and the cartographer depicts a few houses that still survive. But the all-embracing description – the Hundred of Blackheath – comes as something of a surprise.

With places that are as far off as Sydenham this is greatly at odds with our idea of Blackheath, and one explanation of the long twisting boundary is to be found in the *Domesday Book* and goes back even earlier. According to Lambarde Alfred divided the country into thirty-two shires. Kent was one and, like the other shires, was sub-divided into smaller parts called Lathes, Tidings and Hundreds – the latter so named because they 'contained jurisdiction over a hundred pledges' the allegiance of a hundred families.

Hundreds were working administrative units with courts that assembled in the open air on open ground often by a boundary stone, ancient burial mound or some other prominent feature. Almost certainly the Hundred of Blackheath court met on the Heath, and, because the spot is very old, it probably did so at the mound now known as Whitefield's Mount.

In 1571 Lambarde recorded that Blackheath Hundred consisted of seven parishes and their relative importance may be judged from the payments they made towards general upkeep. Lewisham made the largest contribution; Eltham came next and, in descending order, East Greenwich, West Greenwich, Lee, Charlton, Woolwich and Kidbrooke. Even though it qualified as a Hundred, Blackheath had not yet the status of a parish. By 1778 – the date of Hasted's map – the Heath was owned in varying proportions by the Lords of the Manors of Greenwich, Lewisham, Charlton and Kidbrooke and was common land for those parishes.

ROMAN GREENWICH

There was natural local excitement in 1902 when workmen found some tessellated paving and fragments of Roman tiles in a north-eastern dip of Greenwich Park. The park superintendent, A.D. Webster, dug a trial trench, and he is probably the bearded figure in the photograph (3) surveying the site which yielded varied fragmented treasures.

The *Daily Graphic* published drawings of several of these finds (2). The range of dates of other objects stretched from 35 BC (a denarius of Mark Antony's legion) to AD 41-54 (a coin of Claudius I). Even rarer was a find belonging to the reign of Constantine the Great. They came from a buried building which at first was assumed to be a Roman villa. Enthusiasts, however, wanted to push the possibilities further. Could this be the settlement of Noviomagus, the never-located city that might have been in this locality?

A diagonal route across a map of the park from the Shooters Hill end of Watling Street (at the modern Standard public house) to the supposed villa ran in a straight line. Did this not suggest that this was a true extension of Watling Street rather than the long-accepted route across the Heath to the south of the park? Was this the way Julius Caesar marched in 54 BC and possibly crossed the Thames at Greenwich?

3. *Surveying the site in 1902.*

These seductive possibilities ignored the practical realities that at the bottom of the hill this road would have run straight into a marshy foreshore. A wide, deep and fast-flowing river would have made a crossing difficult and progress to London would have been barred by the Deptford Creek end of the Ravensbourne river.

The new Watling Street theory had keen advocates and they were encouraged by further indications of a Roman road discovered with modern laying of gas mains. But even the most credulous are forced to discard Noviomagus and accept the verdict of Dr Ralph Merrifield. The greatest authority on Roman London considers that the discovered artefacts did not signify a villa, but agrees there were enough religious objects to suggest the kind of small Roman temple that was often remotely sited.

2. *The discovery of Roman remains in Greenwich Park was announced in the Daily Graphic. Three of the finds are depicted here. A is part of a Roman statue, B, some decorated ware, and C is a large iron key.*

THE ROMAN VILLA AT GREENWICH.

A SKELETON HISTORY.

Some months ago the DAILY GRAPHIC announced that excavations in Greenwich Park had found some Roman remains which might prove of import... remains, which have accumulated si... are now been ex...

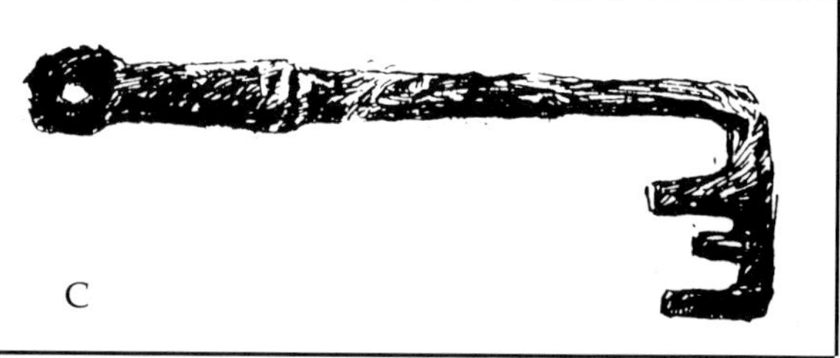

4. Ancient Crooms Hill leading from Blackheath down to Greenwich, as it looked in 1829. Painting by R.W. Lucas.

DARK AGE THEORIES

For centuries after the departure of the Romans around 410 information about Greenwich is sparse. Only intermittent bursts of archaeology came to the help of suspect chronicles and legends about the Dark Ages.

In 1784 a clergyman with a keen antiquarian curiosity, the Revd James Douglas, obtained permission to excavate about fifty puzzling burial mounds, conical and circular, in the park. Douglas made notes of eighteen barrows which he opened. From the largest he recovered 'one of the largest iron spearheads I ever found; fifteen inches long and two broad to the socket...' There was an iron knife and fragments of a metal shield boss. Disappointingly there were no remains of bones, but, he noted, 'on a line where the body seemed to have been laid [was] a considerable quantity of fine vegetable mould; probably decomposed particles of some wooden case in which the corpse had been deposited.' From another tumulus, crossed by Crooms Hill, Douglas also brought to light a braid of auburn-coloured human hair, beads and pieces of cloth which showed weave marks and a herring-bone pattern.

Limited though these discoveries were, they were sufficiently evocative of pomp and ceremony to suggest that they might have a connection with the early Saxon kings of Kent dating back to Hengest in the fifth century. This could not, of course, be confirmed, and no documentary evidence about Greenwich (spelt Grenewye and Gronovic) exists before the ninth century and the reign of King Alfred.

After he became King of the West Saxons in 871 Alfred allotted some part of his Gronovic property to the Abbey of Ghent as well as giving a holding to his daughter Elftrudis – perhaps as a marriage portion – and on the death of her husband in 918 Elftrudis added her part of this Greenwich gift to Ghent.

Many centuries later the grant and bequest of Alfred and his daughter came back into English hands. The story is a tortuous one but important because the 'manor', or 'manoir' as it is referred to, was developed into a great house by the river in the Middle Ages and, more importantly still, that same great house was converted into a palace by the Tudors.

5. Martyrdom of St Alphege. 12th-century window in Canterbury Cathedral.

THE MURDER OF ALPHEGE

Dark Age uncertainties take definite historical shape in the eleventh century when, as Lambarde records, 'the whole fleete of the Danish army lay at roade two or three yeeres together before Greenewich: And the souldiors, for the most part, were incamped upon the hille above the towne, now called Blackheath'.

From their camp on the Heath the Danes ravaged the whole country and in 1011 besieged Canterbury which fell after twenty days. Archbishop Alphege was brought to Greenwich by a ship on which he and others were imprisoned and half starved for seven months. The Danes demanded a ransom, a promise of which may have been given and then rescinded: as Lambarde put it, Alphege would not 'condescend' to redeem his life with the money the people of Canterbury were prepared to put up.

In a frenzy after a drunken feast the Danes killed their captive and Lambarde adds the curious note that a Dane named Thrum who struck Alphege from behind had been confirmed as a Christian by him only the previous day. Lambarde also recounts that the Danes would not let the body be buried until a dead stick smeared with his blood became green and blossomed – the sort of miracle, the historian adds sarcastically, with which 'our ancient monkish stories do swarme'.

This is the scene depicted in a twelfth-century stained glass window at Canterbury (5). The Danes are said to have flung stones, wood and ox skulls, remnants of the feast, at the Archbishop. This brought him to the ground and the convert decided to put him out of his agony with his axe.

Another 'monkish' footnote was that there were many Christian converts among the Danes, and for this reason Alphege's body was allowed to be taken reverently to London for burial at St Paul's before final interment at Canterbury eleven years later.

St Alphege's Church in the centre of Greenwich is a memorial to the Archbishop and tradition has it that the church stands on the place of his martyrdom, and the tradition is an old one for there has been a church on the site since the twelfth century. The present Hawksmoor building dates from the reign of Queen Anne following a storm in 1710. This was when an earlier church which had served the town, palace and Court was destroyed.

6. John Ball inciting the peasants to attack the principal lords of England. Ms drawing from Froissart's Chroniques de France et Angleterre, *c.1460.*

GREENWICH IN DOMESDAY

In the Domesday Book of 1086 three entries mention holdings in Grenviz (i.e. Greenwich) Hundred. The one of most interest alludes to land held by the Abbot of Gand (i.e. Ghent) which must refer to the ancient grant to Ghent made by Alfred the Great and his daughter (p.11). The land in their Greenwich Hundred is described as 'Levesha.' (i.e. Lewisham). There is mention of a revenue of forty shillings from the Port which suggests that Greenwich, actually on the Thames, is included in the Lewisham category. There is a reference to thirty acres of meadow but most interesting of all is the existence of eleven mills. These must have been on and driven by the Ravensbourne river and it is plausible that these are ancient versions of Mumford's Mill at Deptford, recently demolished, and the still existing mill which houses the National Portrait Gallery archives behind the Riverdale Centre in Lewisham.

EVENTS ON BLACKHEATH

Close to London, and on the direct road from the coast, Blackheath was a natural place for ceremonial events. Civic dignitaries came here to greet royalty and flatter important foreign visitors. It was a natural amphitheatre for pageantry and celebrations. The Heath was suited for political demonstrations and famous preachers selected it for religious meetings.

Rebels made their ragged way to Blackheath, and earliest among them were followers of Wat Tyler, the Dartford blacksmith, and the priest Jack Straw, who in 1381 assembled 100,000 malcontents to protest against the poll tax. Almost no contemporary pictures record this or other uprisings but a manuscript drawing (6) shows John Ball, the rebellious priest who helped the incitement. On a horse, he is delivering a sermon on equality to Tyler's men with the potent text: 'When Adam delved and Eve span / Who was then the gentleman?' Ball is remembered today by a school named after him on the north side of the Heath and by a mound covered in trees. This mound was identified by Lambarde as Wat Tyler's Mount. As well as being the legendary spot where Tyler, the blacksmith, set up his forge and tent, it is also known as Whitefield's Mount – the place chosen by George Whitefield, the eighteenth-century Calvinist preacher, to address a vast open air congregation.

In the fourteenth century there was the first of the many receptions on Blackheath given by London's lord mayors and officials to welcome home a king – on this occasion Richard II – who had returned from abroad with a wife who promised a profitable alliance. In 1400 Henry IV welcomed the Emperor of Constantinople – a meeting which marked the first stage in an alliance against the Turks. The long roll of events stretches out to include the City's welcome to Henry V fifteen years later when some 20,000 Londoners, nobles and City fathers 'mounted and clothed in scarlet' came to acclaim his Agincourt victory.

The Agincourt demonstration was unusual because apparently Henry did not welcome his reception. The occasion was dampened by the King's reluctance to accept 'such vaine pompe and shewes as were in triumphant sort devised for his welcoming home' (Holinshed). He refused to have his helmet carried before him as a symbol of his victory and minstrels despondently returned to London without singing vainglorious ditties they had prepared. Nevertheless later in the century, when the Emperor of Germany came to negotiate a peace between England and France, Henry was on Blackheath to greet him. On this occasion he was accompanied by Humphrey, Duke of Gloucester. Humphrey again played welcoming host when he was delegated to meet Margaret of Anjou at Blackheath on her arrival for her coronation in 1445. He took the opportunity to invite her down to the house he had been given on the river at Greenwich. There was a prophetic irony in this; when Humphrey fell from grace and died two years later Margaret wasted no time in appropriating his Greenwich property.

7. William Lambarde (1536-1601), the Greenwich historian, inherited the manor of Westcombe from his father, a City draper and sheriff, in 1554 and died there in 1601. The first draft of his Perambulation of Kent *(8) was written in 1570. Lambarde lived in this house facing west towards modern Vanbrugh Hill only intermittently. He was at Greenwich for Elizabeth I's celebration of Maundy in 1573. A rich man as well as a scholar and historian, he founded the still-existing almshouse in Greenwich.*

Before the next royal occasion the Heath was again the scene of revolt. Jack Cade, the Irish-born rebel who lived in Kent, encamped with 40,000 followers and prepared the 'Blackheath Petition' asking for a redress of grievances before going on to London. After various outrages and Cade's violent death, his followers returned to the Heath 'naked save their shirts' and knelt to receive the King's pardon.

When a force of Cornishmen marched on London in 1495 – yet another protest against taxes – they were engaged in a pitched battle against Henry VII's army and out of 6,000 men from the West Country as many as 2,000 are reported to have been killed. The Heath was their graveyard.

After this tragedy Blackheath saw a return to the glitter and pomp of royal occasions. In the next century the most impressive was Henry VIII's first ceremonial meeting with Anne of Cleves. Tents and pavilions were put up on the east side of the Heath and, for a meeting which sounds like a re-run of the Field of the Cloth of Gold, he and his future bride enjoyed a sumptuous picnic. The ceremony ended when Henry, dressed in purple and gold set with jewels, led Anne down to his palace at Greenwich along a triumphal pathway cut through the gorse.

8. Title page of the 19th-century reprint of Lambarde's book.

PERAMBULATION

OF

KENT:

CONTEINING THE

DESCRIPTION, HYSTORIE, AND CUSTOMES

OF

That Shire.

WRITTEN IN THE YEERE 1570,

By William Lambarde, of Lincolnes Inne, Gent:

First published in the Year 1576,

And now increased and altered from the Author's owne last Copie.

Chatham:

PRINTED BY W. BURRILL, HIGH-STREET;

PUBLISHED BY BALDWIN, CRADOCK, AND JOY, PATERNOSTER-ROW, LONDON;

And may be had of all other Booksellers.

1826.

9. Hollar's view of Duke Humphrey's Tower in the seventeenth century.

BELLA COURT AND HUMPHREY'S TOWER

From Lambarde we have the nearest contemporary account by a historian of the foundation of the Greenwich estate which in the next hundred years was to develop into the great Tudor palace of Placentia. By 1433 the holding had passed from the Abbey of St Peter at Ghent back to the Crown and was granted by Henry VI to his uncle Humphrey, Duke of Gloucester.

Humphrey immediately set about developing one building and creating another. He converted the Abbey premises into 'a faire building in the towne' - Old Court by the river – which he later called Bella Court; the other was 'a toure in the Park', a formidable square fortress on the overlooking hill.

At the same time he acquired 200 acres of Blackheath which he enclosed with a fence of wooden stakes; this was in outline the future Greenwich Park.

The two buildings could hardly have been more different. Bella Court, built of rose-pink brick and lavishly furnished, contained the magnificent library which Duke Humphrey was to leave to the Bodleian, Oxford. This represented the aesthetic and scholarly side of Humphrey's character. Nothing remains of this house above ground but excavations in 1970-71 established its position as being just to the west of the present Royal Naval College.

The tower, sometimes called Greenwich Castle, symbolized the Humphrey who had fought at Agincourt and captured Lisieux. He planned it as a lookout and defensive stronghold against attack on London by an enemy coming up the Thames or by land from the Channel ports. Its strength was never tested and there are only imprecise views of how it looked as a castle. Wenceslaus Hollar shows the tower as it appeared in 1637 (9) before it was demolished, by which time it was more residential than martial.

Within a fortnight of Duke Humphrey's death in 1447 Bella Court was given to Margaret of Anjou, Henry VI's young wife, a girl of seventeen. She made considerable alterations over a period of five years and changed the name to 'Pleasunce'.

Edward IV and his queen, Elizabeth Woodville, enlarged the manor but tantalizingly no picture exists of the house. It seems that despite all improvements the old house was almost completely destroyed in about 1500 and 600,000 bricks purchased for the rebuilding by Henry VII.

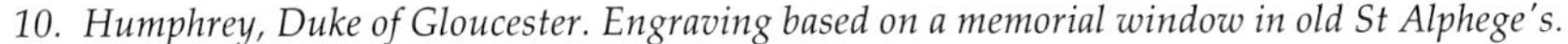

10. Humphrey, Duke of Gloucester. Engraving based on a memorial window in old St Alphege's.

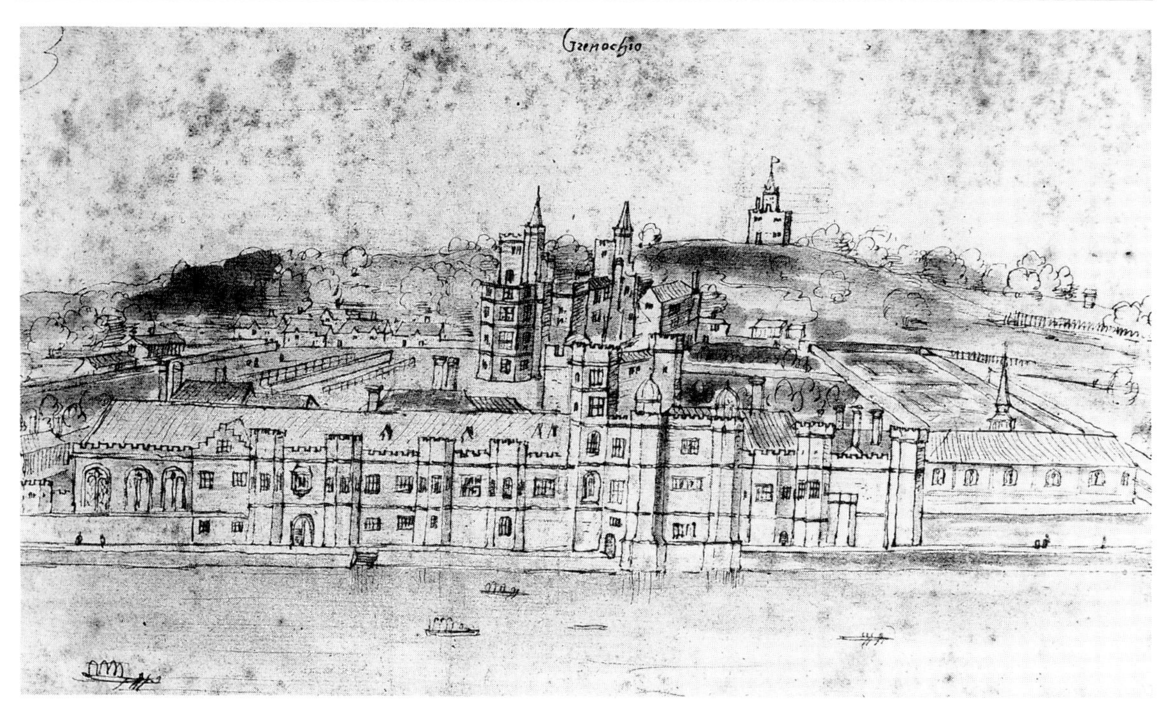

11. Greenwich Palace from the north, by Anthony van den Wyngaerde.

12. River view. 19th-century print based on an early 17th-century painting by an unknown artist.

Tudor and Stuart Greenwich

PLACENTIA

A royal palace rose in all its glory on the Greenwich waterfront at the beginning of the sixteenth century. Henry VII was responsible for the initial transformation and extension of Bella Court, and, Lambarde recorded, he refaced and rebuilt the old structure. This became Placentia, one of the greatest of Tudor palaces and was to exist for 160 years.

Henry VII's building took six years to complete. Dominated by a tower that extended over the water, the palace stretched for a hundred yards from east to west. The King's Bedchamber was in the main tower probably on the first floor, and also overlooking the curve of the Thames were the main private rooms and audience chambers.

An unknown artist of the early seventeenth century shows the front view with red brick facade, turrets and crenellated parapet, and for the fullest comprehensive picture of how Placentia was to develop over the next century Anthony van den Wyngaerde, an artist from the Low Countries, provides two bird's-eye-views of the rambling buildings which stretch back from the Thames to the edge of the park that was the royal hunting ground.

14. Henry VIII, from a painting by Holbein.

Henry VIII was born in the palace which was his boyhood home and remained his favourite palace outside London after he became king in 1509. In the

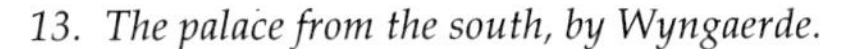

13. The palace from the south, by Wyngaerde.

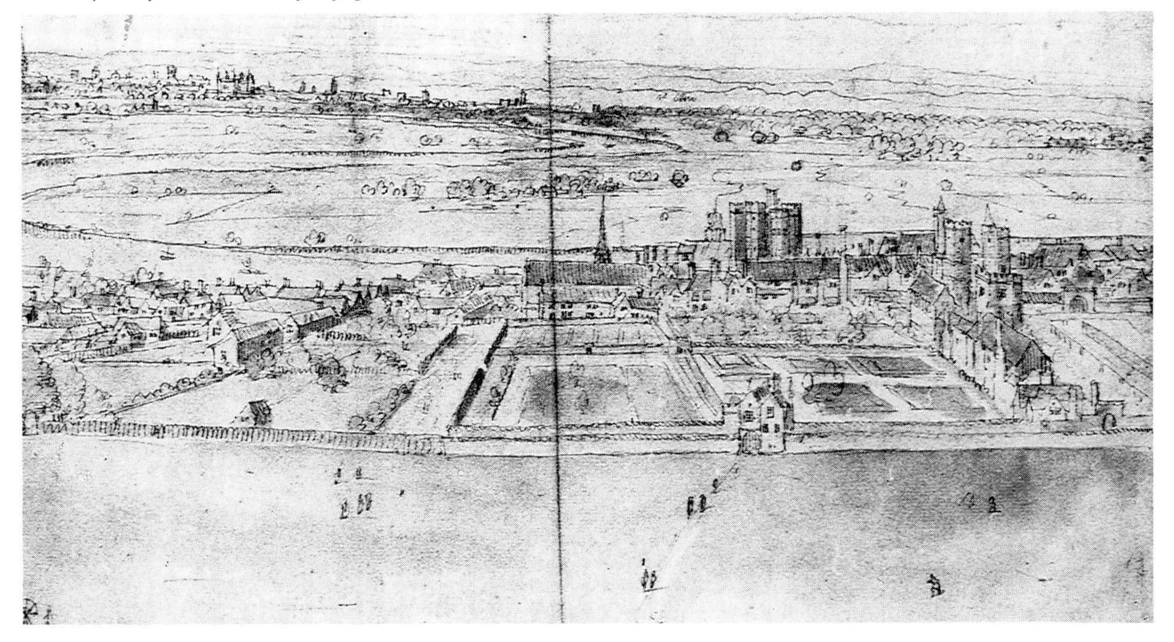

15. Placentia from Oak Tree Hill in the early 1600s, by an unknown artist whose perspective of the palace is deceptive.

16. 'Challenge at Castle' 1524. A Christmas entertainment.

year of his accession he extended the building started by his father with an eye to greater pleasure. Keen horseman and skilled jouster, he built a tiltyard and stables which Wyngaerde shows and also a building to seat spectators.

Tournaments were not confined to the tiltyard. Henry devised variations. One Christmas he had a mock castle erected surrounded by a moat where supposed lady prisoners were held captive by a captain and fifteen gentlemen against the assault of all-comers. This was varied at another Christmas entertainment when a tower was built in the Great Hall. Again the theme was gallantry; with five companions Henry, dressed in satin and cloth of gold, rescued six ladies.

Greenwich was the constant setting for ingenious devices, and in a symbolic tableau staged for the French ambassador in 1518 a lady was discovered sitting on a rock, a dolphin in her lap. Knights emerged

from caves to fight for her release, and their success was said to symbolize the victory of Christianity over Evil.

Sometimes the scale of hospitality at Placentia strained even the resources of the many-chambered building. When Catherine of Aragon's nephew, Charles V, arrived in 1522 his retinue was so large that the town was asked for help with accommodation. The people of Greenwich managed to produce 129 beds and stabling for eighty-eight horses.

The birth of a daughter Elizabeth to Henry's second wife, Anne Boleyn, marked the start of the next great period in Placentia's history. Repeating his own christening, Henry arranged for her to be baptized at Greenwich, and Elizabeth grew to love Placentia. It became her favourite palace of which she wrote: 'Sure the house, garden and walks may compare with the most delicat in Italy'.

From her windows overlooking the river she saw the start and conclusion of important events. She watched Martin Frobisher sail down the Thames at the outset of his search for the North West Passage. On a particularly memorable day the *Golden Hind* sailed up the river and she received Francis Drake to hear of his circumnavigation of the world. She went aboard for the ceremony of his knighthood.

On a black day at Greenwich the Queen put her reluctant signature to the death warrant of Mary, Queen of Scots. In the perilous days when the Armada threatened it was from her council chamber that she gave orders for England's resistance.

At Greenwich during the Christmas festivities in 1594 Shakespeare made his first officially recorded appearance as an actor. The play performed by the Lord Chamberlain's Men was probably *The Comedy of Errors* which they were to repeat the next night at Gray's Inn.

In the varied tapestry of events there is a droll charm about the visit of Grace O'Malley, the pirate Queen of Connaught, who arrived at Placentia without any English to find Elizabeth spoke no Gaelic. They solved the problem by speaking in Latin.

A picture of the Queen at her river home late in her life comes from a German visitor who in 1598 speaks of her 'in the sixty-fifth year of her age as we are told, very majestic...Her air was stately, her manner of speaking mild and obliging...' Yet another visitor was the Greenwich historian Lambarde who, appointed keeper of the Tower of London, records he came to show her his account. This was in 1601, two years before her death.

17. *Anne of Cleves.*

18. Aerial view of the Royal Naval College and the Queen's House, overlaid with a conjectural plan of Placentia.

PLACENTIA REVEALED

Excavations in the Grand Square of the Royal Naval College were carried out by the Department of the Environment in 1970-71. Their findings, combined with Wyngaerde's views of 1558 and contemporary building accounts, now make it possible to plot a conjectural Tudor Palace of Greenwich in relation to existing buildings.

The most privileged private and ceremonial apartments overlooked the river and ranged for about 100 yards from the Chapel Royal (4) to the Privy Kitchen (9) – the kitchen identified by three large fireplaces discovered during excavations. On the first floor were the Presence Chamber (5) where the sovereign met important visitors; the long Privy Chamber (6) reserved for conferences with the Privy Council; and the King's Bedchamber (7). Probably one floor up was the 'highest library' (8), an outstanding collection of books formed after 1519 by Henry VIII.

Several of these important rooms were in the tall central tower projecting over the Thames – shown by Wyngaerde. They looked out on three courtyards away from the river; the main Inner Court (1), Middle Court (2) and Chapel Court (3). Among many royal apartments, opening on to each other or linked by galleries, was the Queen's Bedchamber (10) and, further round the Inner Court on the south, rooms were designated as 'the Queen's lodgings' (11).

An important part of the palace until the Reformation was the Church of the Observant Friars (12) founded in 1487. Here Henry VIII was baptized and married Catherine of Aragon, and Elizabeth was baptized and confirmed as a baby in 1533, the year before the suppression of the Franciscan monks.

Between the Middle and Chapel courtyards stood the Great Hall (13) of which a vaulted seventeenth-century undercroft survives beneath the present Queen Anne building. Used for early Tudor festivities this timber-framed building was probably superseded when the Banqueting House (14) was created between two octagonal towers in 1527 as part of a 300-yard promontory to the south of the palace. It was built at the same time as the Disguising House (15), another name for a theatre, which had a musicians' gallery, and seats which could be laid out on three sides like an amphitheatre. These two buildings were linked by the Tiltyard Gallery (16) from which spectators watched a series of spectacular tournaments in the Tiltyard (17) built in 1515 by Henry who, from the age of nineteen, was a jousting champion who took on all challengers. The building to the south (stretching across present Romney Road and lawns of the National Maritime Museum) were outside the 1970s' excavations, but Wyngaerde's view (p.17) shows it clearly and also the gatehouse (18) leading into Greenwich Park, the Great Garden (19) and the Orchard (20).

19. James I. Drawn by Laurence Johnson, 1603.

CHANGES UNDER JAMES I

For a decade after Queen Elizabeth's death Greenwich went into the doldrums. The palace had been neglected towards the end of the Queen's reign and some of her courtiers and advisers had drifted away. Many belonged to famous families. They left behind houses built during the century when Greenwich Palace had been the bustling centre of Court life. After the departure of the Courtenay family, one of the largest, Swanne House (on the site of the modern enclosed market), fell into the hands of successive speculators. The Dudleys, whose mansion was near the royal stables, had gone; so, too, had the Greys, marquesses of Dorset, and the Comptons whose orchards and gardens reached from the river to the park. Their once fine houses were divided up and dropped on the social scale.

One great name remained. Henry Howard, Earl of Northampton, who had been brought up in a lodge in the park, retained his family's old interest in the town. In 1604 he acquired Old Court, the former manorial name for the palace, from Sir Robert Cecil who had obtained it from James I at the start of his reign. Howard spent more than £2,000 putting buildings and land 'in good plight' and made his home in Greenwich Castle – as Duke Humphrey's Tower was now called – which had acquired a domestic look. His enthusiasm extended to keeping up the surrounding park and to taking over a house on the river, formerly owned by Lord Lumley. This he was to convert into Trinity Hospital which still exists as an almshouse.

These varied changes marked the imprecise status of Greenwich when James I arrived from Scotland and had to decide where near London he wished to live. The Old Palace at Theobalds in Hertfordshire appealed to him most but, without appearing to do so, he wanted to keep in check the acquisitive tendencies of those round Greenwich Palace. This he managed by allowing his queen, Anne of Denmark, to take back the park under the Crown. This plan thwarted Howard's ambitions, and he fired off letters of protest and bemoaned that 'Her Majesty will not find a servant to keep with so much tenderness as I have done the ground and the deer and the little wood that is left there'. He protested in vain. His Greenwich holdings were granted by James to Anne for 100 years – adding the wry proviso 'should she live so long'.

The disconsolate Howard left Greenwich and died within months in London, but, in part reparation for his rights being lost, his nephew and heir was permitted to occupy the castle on the hill, and lived there for twenty years. Down in the town the Howards' Old Court mansion was taken over by his nephew Thomas Howard, Earl of Arundel. Here he kept his art

20. Anne of Denmark.

collection while Arundel House, off the Strand, was being prepared for the treasures bought on his travels abroad.

While still at Greenwich part of his collection was destroyed by a fire. Fortunately the treasures had been catalogued and their value assessed shortly before by Inigo Jones, who had been on the Earl's Italian tours to buy works of art.

This is the first mention of Inigo Jones's connection with Greenwich, but it appears that in 1616 the architect leased a house called Blew Boar on the river (on the site of the Ship Tavern) – a strange arrangement because Jones sold it the next day to Arundel. It would certainly have made an ideal place from which to supervise his project of the following year.

A 'CURIOUS DEVICE'

The first intimation of what Jones was up to comes in a letter from the valuable gossip John Chamberlain to his friend Sir Dudley Carleton. Chamberlain wrote: 'The Queen...is building somewhat in Greenwich which must be finished this summer; it is said to be a curious device by Inigo Jones and will cost above £4,000.' This rather deprecating phrase is the first mention of the earliest classical domestic building in England.

Curious in many ways the house must have seemed. For a start, the architect had the whimsical notion of making it span a road – the highway from Greenwich to Woolwich – so that the Queen had unimpeded access both to the park to the south and the old palace by the river to the north. It was on this muddy road between high walls that legend has Sir Walter Raleigh laying down his cloak to prevent Queen Elizabeth stepping in a puddle.

But odder still was the style of the house. Jones based his design on villas by Andrea Palladio and Vincenzo Scamozzi which he had admired on his visits to Italy in the company of Arundel. In contrast to the palace and the new brick architecture of the time, the proposed house was finished in white

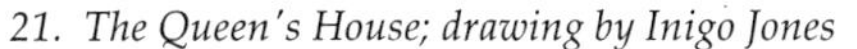

21. The Queen's House; drawing by Inigo Jones

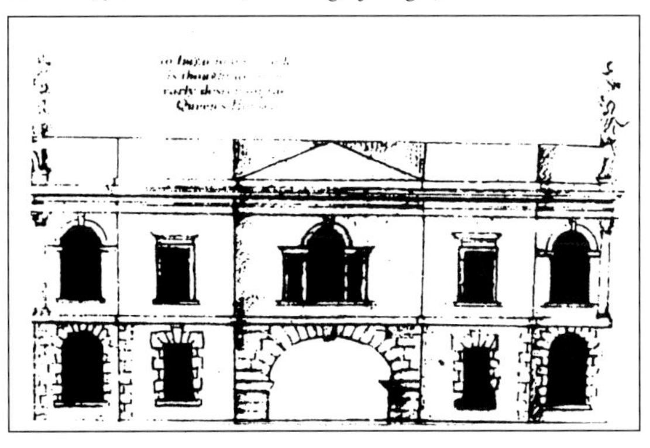

22. Inigo Jones; by Hollar after Van Dyck.

23. Sketch by Inigo Jones of the Queen's House.

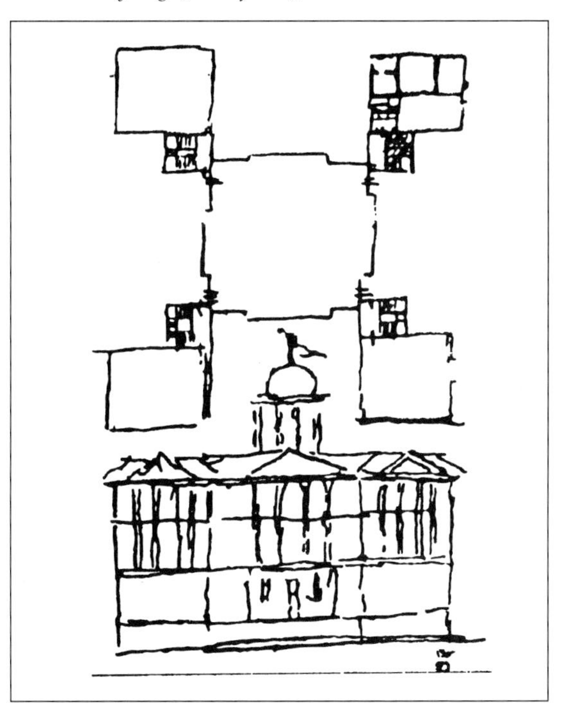

24. Charles I and Henrietta Maria with their family and courtiers. The uncompleted Queen's House is in the middle distance of this painting by an unknown artist.

25. *The Queen's House; engraving by Thomas Morris, 1791.*

26. *Henrietta Maria*

cement. Tall windows with large square panes were used instead of leaded Tudor ones. A loggia overlooking the park had Ionic columns. The scale of the building was modest, the proportions symmetrical. This neat little doll's house was a daring innovation soon to be referred to as the 'House of Delight'.

To start with, Inigo Jones may not have planned anything quite so radical. A sketch attributed to him shows (23) that he first proposed corner pavilions which would have been at odds with the classical simplicity. Another sketch shows a road archway of the kind planned to join the two blocks of his H-shaped building (21).

Chamberlain's letter said the house was due to be finished in the summer of 1617 but it was still not completed when the Queen died in 1619. Work had stopped when she became ill the previous year. It is not certain what stage building had reached; perhaps the ideas for corner pavilions died with her.

Three years later James handed Greenwich over to his son Charles, and after his succession Charles gave the unfinished house to his French wife, Henrietta Maria. Jones resumed work in 1629 and completion is recorded on a tablet over the central window: 'Henrica Maria Regina 1635'. She furnished it lavishly and artists were commissioned to paint panels and the decorative ceiling in the Great Hall.

A chance to see the house is given by the artist who shows the building (24) apparently still only at first floor level on a day when Charles I, Henrietta Maria and their family have climbed the hill in the park with their courtiers. In the background, the old palace stands gaunt by the river and screened by trees that have grown up since Wyngaerde drew the ornamental gardens. The small gatehouse has been demolished to make way for houses and a high wall marks the north boundary of the park along the line of the old road. This is part of the two-mile wall with which James replaced the wooden fencing and enclosed the park.

Externally the Queen's House has changed little over the years, and its tranquil simplicity is perfectly conveyed in a late eighteenth-century engraving (25). In the foreground are tame deer, always a feature of the park and today kept in an enclosure appropriately called the Wilderness.

When James died the Surveyor General, John Webb, was asked to make the house less cramped. Webb wanted to be faithful to his predecessor's plan, so instead of building on a new wing which would have destroyed the shape, he added two new bridges to retain the proportions. The bridges turned the H into a square and gave Henrietta Maria two fine additional salons. These she only briefly enjoyed before the Civil War forced her to take refuge in France. During the Commonwealth when the main palace suffered indignities, the house escaped damage because Cromwell gave it to one of his counsellors and it was mainly kept for official use.

The house was given a facelift in 1990 (27), and in an endeavour to recapture the interior appearance the royal apartments have been refurnished as they might have been after the Restoration when the Dowager Queen was in residence. The modern furnishings and colours conform as far as possible to an inventory of possessions taken at her death in 1669.

27. The restored hallway of the Queen's House.

At the Restoration

29. *Charles II; engraving from a portrait by Sir Peter Lely.*

For Charles II Blackheath was the last and most important stage of his journey to London at the Restoration. After landing at Dover on 25 May 1660 and an overnight stay at Rochester he left his coach for horseback and was greeted on the Heath by the army. This had been drawn up by General Monck who, though he had served Cromwell, was anxious for the restoration of the old order.

Bareheaded, Charles waved to morris dancers who were part of a vast concourse of 120,000 waiting to greet him. The Lord Mayor, Thomas Alleyn, was at the bottom of Blackheath Hill, ready to accompany him into London.

The King's first visit to Greenwich Palace after his return was not propitious. The long-locked entrance gates had to be broken open and, when he walked round them, the deserted, uncared-for buildings hardly inspired plans for repair. But as Samuel Pepys noted, the King liked the setting facing the river and John Webb, the Surveyor General, was told to start work on a new palace.

Five years later money ran out with only one wing partially completed. After that the old palace stood empty for the next twenty years with half-ruined buildings falling further into decay.

28. *Remains of Duke Humphrey's Tower, demolished to build the Observatory.*

30. *The Royal Observatory from Crooms Hill, 1680; oil painting, artist unknown.*

31. The Octagon Room in the Royal Observatory.

ROYAL OBSERVATORY

The pleasures of Whitehall had not completely swept Greenwich from Charles II's mind and it was in 1675 that he made the momentous decision to build an observatory there. Up on the hill in Greenwich Park were the ruins of Duke Humphrey's defensive tower – a jagged stump if an undated engraving (28) is to be believed.

He ordered that rubble from the tower should provide some of the foundations for the building which Wren was to design. Alternative sites in Hyde Park and Chelsea were rejected in favour of Greenwich, 150 feet up and with unimpeded views.

The King's warrant was simple and clear:

'Whereas, in order to the finding out of the longitude of places for perfecting navigation and astronomy, we have resolved to build a small observatory within Our Park at Greenwich upon the highest ground at or near the place where the castle stood...'.

The need for an observatory was pressing but the way it came about was devious and smacks of petticoat influence.

The important navigational help that sailors required at the time was to be able to fix their position at sea – their 'longitude' – and this could only be

32. Louise de Keroualle, Duchess of Portsmouth; from the studio of Sir Peter Lely.

achieved by observing the position of the moon in relation to the stars. A way of doing this had been advanced by a Frenchman who styled himself Le Sieur de St Pierre. Little is known about St Pierre except that he was a friend of the Duchess of Portsmouth, the former Louise de Kerouaille who, recently naturalized, had become the King's mistress and by whom he had a son.

Such a source – a French Catholic – was inevitably resented. John Flamsteed, a rising young astronomer, slightingly described St Pierre as 'having some small skill in astronomy' but the King was insistent. He said he did not want 'his ship-owners and sailors deprived of any help the Heavens could provide' and appointed a Royal Commission to examine the Frenchman's theories.

Because readings would take many years an observatory was essential. Wren set about the design 'for the Observator's habitation' to be built, as he put it, 'a little for pompe'.

The doll's house-sized living quarters, like Flamsteed's annual salary (£100) as Astronomer Royal, were certainly not grand. But the Octagonal Room above was one of Wren's happiest creations (31). Here in 1676 Flamsteed 'began to observe ye heavens'. On the far wall, below a portrait of Charles II, there were, as a seventeenth-century print shows, two clocks made by Thomas Tompion. Concealed behind a panelled wainscot were pendulums, thirteen feet long for accuracy. These clocks were used by the astronomer to check the regularity of the earth's rotation. There was a sextant, a quadrant and four telescopes, one of which, fifty-two feet long, is seen suspended diagonally from a tall mast (33).

The Observatory, with rose-pink bricks, white quoins, little cupolas and tall windows with views over the river was – and remains – almost theatrically effective. But the most important observations requiring the fundamental instruments – a sextant and mural arc – were carried out in a more mundane outbuilding in Flamsteed's garden. Here he made almost 50,000 observations and catalogued the stars

34. John Flamsteed and assistant. Detail from the Thornhill painted ceiling in the Painted Hall, Greenwich.

and other heavenly bodies in his task of solving the longitude problem. St Pierre was quickly discomfited by Flamsteed who wrote '...he huffed a little and disappeared; since which time we have heard no further from him'. But at least this sketchily known Frenchman was the instigator, all unknowingly, of the Royal Observatory.

Flamsteed's great work spread over forty-four years to produce an almanack of the moon and stars. His *Stellarum* was published posthumously in 1725. It was an achievement that involved a great deal of controversy and heartache during his lifetime, but his definitive information was to lead, indirectly, to Greenwich being accepted as the 'prime meridian' – Longitude 0 – and the division of the world into Eastern and Western hemispheres with their variation in time. Calculating time from Greenwich was increasingly accepted after 1884 until Greenwich Mean Time was superseded by the atomic clock.

33. Prospect of London and the Observatory; etching by Francis Place.

TIME BALL AND TIME LADY

An outward display of Greenwich Time came in 1833 when the Admiralty ordered that a ball should be dropped daily at 1.00 p.m. from the top of a pole on the Observatory. This was to enable seamen on the river to make a visual check of the time. Nineteen years later a twenty-four hour clock was put up outside the Observatory gate.

Dissemination of the correct time – Greenwich Mean Time – was not easy before radio, and one way in which the difficulty was overcome was shown by Ruth Belville at the end of the century. The daughter of an assistant at the Observatory, Miss Belville carried out a service started by her father. Every Monday morning she took her silver chronometer (nicknamed 'Arnold', after the maker) up to the twenty-four hour clock, checked the time and then made calls on some fifty local clients. 'How's Arnold today?', was their query, to which, if her chronometer was as much as a few seconds fast, she replied, 'Arnold's gay today'.

The adoption of British – that is Greenwich - Time throughout the country helped to keep the country's clocks uniform but it was not until the six pips signal on the wireless was introduced in 1924 that the country as a whole had a time check. 'Arnold' and his like became redundant and with them the services of Miss Belville, the 'Greenwich Time Lady' who died in 1943 aged ninety.

Greenwich Prime Meridian – marked out in cobbles in the courtyard – enables visitors to stand with one foot on either side of Longitude 0 and so in the Eastern and Western hemispheres simultaneously.

36. The exact position of the meridian is marked by a large telescope installed by Sir George Airy, the Astronomer Royal in 1851. Airy's Transit Circle is housed in the 18th-century Meridian Building with a tall stable-like door open for its use. The instrument, shown above, was officially retired in 1954.

35. Edwardian scene: cars and visitors at the Observatory in 1906, waiting for the Time Ball to drop.

37. Ruth Belville making her weekly time check.

Queen Anne and Georgian Greenwich

39. *Self-portrait of James Thornhill which he incorporated in his Painted Hall mural.*

GREENWICH HOSPITAL

Like a spectre at a feast, Greenwich Palace lay empty and falling into decay for several years after William and Mary came to the throne. The Tudor buildings, half-heartedly accepted by James I and Charles I who preferred to live elsewhere, had suffered indignities amounting to desecration during the Commonwealth. Roundhead troops had used the State rooms as barracks and after the Restoration stories were rife of horses being stabled under moulded ceilings and about the way fine works of art had been taken from the walls and sold abroad. According to one report, the palace was reduced to 'a whole heap of rubbish'.

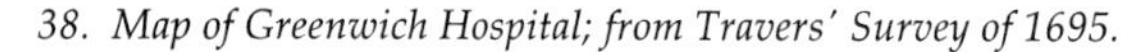

38. *Map of Greenwich Hospital; from Travers' Survey of 1695.*

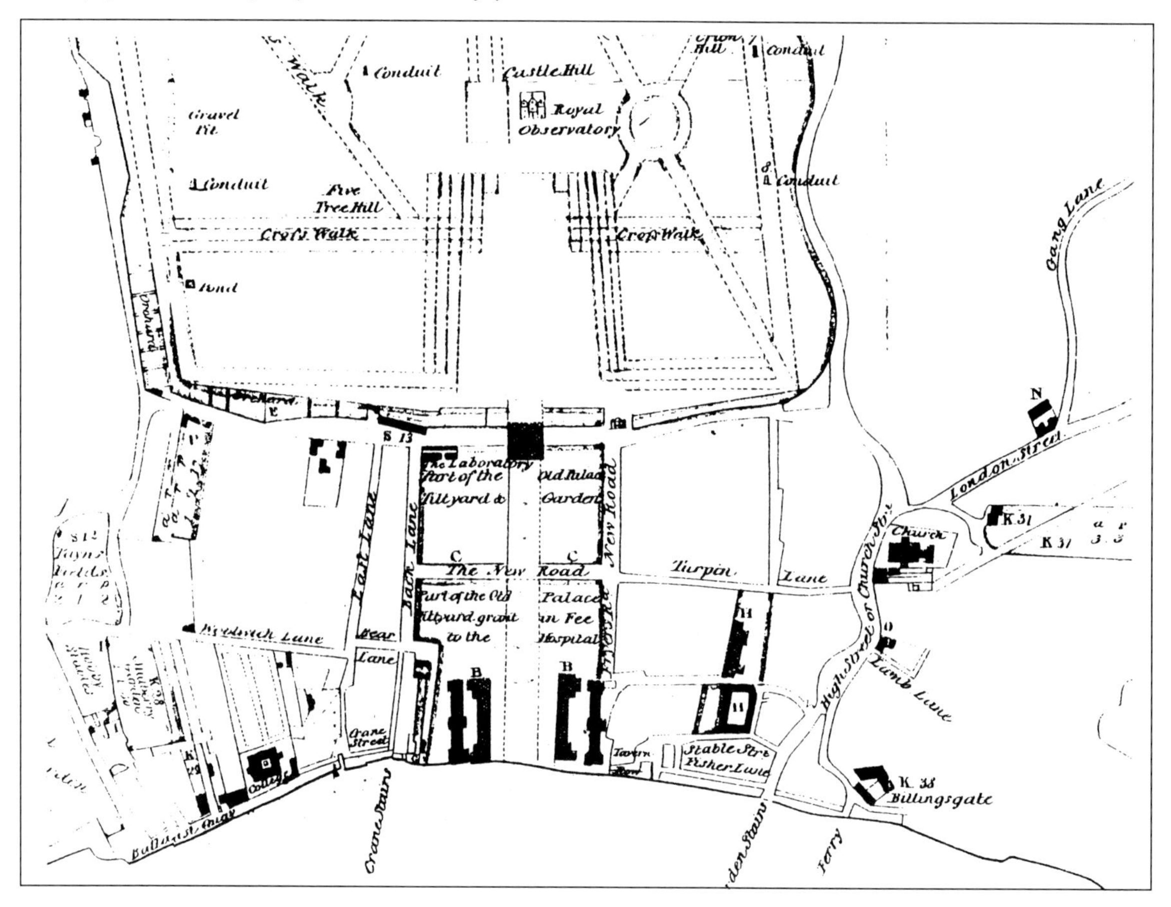

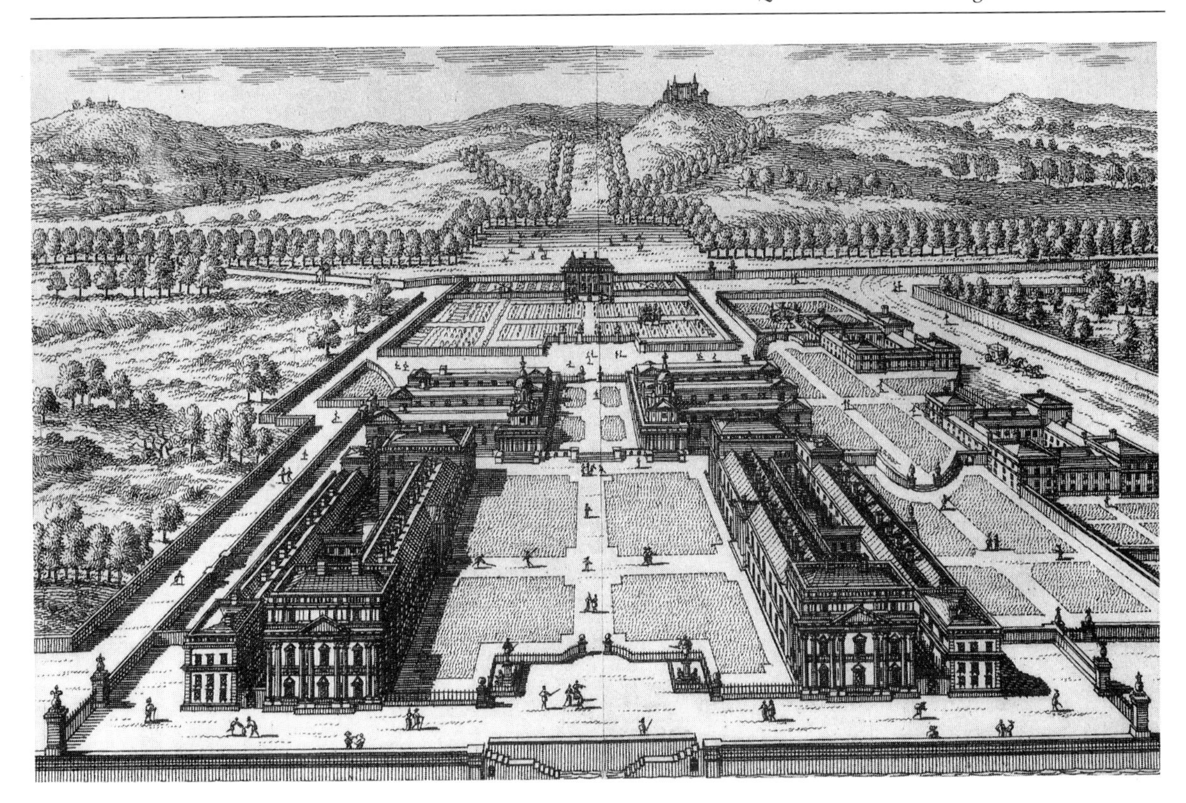

40. *John Kip's View of Greenwich Hospital.*

If Charles II had not favoured Whitehall, Greenwich might have come back into favour. He had given John Webb orders to rebuild but money ran out after five years with only the wing named after him partially completed. After that the old palace stood empty with half-ruined buildings falling further into decay for the next twenty years.

William of Orange suffered from asthma and this made him choose Kensington Palace, well away from the river. Greenwich did not have any place in his or Queen Mary's scheme of things. The Crown

41. *Wren's 'faux-pas' scheme for Greenwich Hospital.*

42. *Sir Christopher Wren.*

43. Carousing pensioners, a cartoon by Isaac Cruikshank.

might easily have given up the palace altogether, but for some time an idea had been in the air for a sailors' hospital. Encouraged by Samuel Pepys, a previous secretary of the Admiralty, and by John Evelyn, who lived at Deptford and was greatly concerned for the care of sick and wounded seaman, the idea gained impetus with the opening of Chelsea Hospital for old soldiers in 1692.

Queen Mary remembered how, as Lord High Admiral, her father, James II, had wanted an institution for the veteran and disabled sailors of the Dutch wars, but his reign had been too short for the plan to become a reality. With only two years to live - she died from smallpox aged thirty-two in 1694 - Mary was busily promoting a home for old sailors, perhaps even larger than Chelsea, as the 'darling object of her life'. Her death, if anything, spurred on the scheme. Backdated to involve her, a charter was issued in the names of both Mary and William for 'an Hospital within Our Mannor of East Greenwich in Our County of Kent for the reliefe and support of Seamen...'

The charter went on to specify that they should be Royal Navy sailors who 'by reason of Age, Wounds

44. Pensioners eating at Greenwich Hospital. Drawn for the Illustrated London News *in 1865.*

45. A colonnade of Greenwich Hospital. Engraving by W.H. Toms.

or other disabilities' were incapable of further service and unable to support themselves. Their widows should be helped and their children educated.

Wren produced a plan. His drawings showed a large domed building linked to flanking wings towards the Thames (41). Unfortunately it was so positioned that the river view of the Queen's House was totally obscured and the house might even have been demolished for all he seemed to care. Queen Mary reacted angrily to this idea. She saw its destruction as an insult to both her grandmother and to Henrietta Maria's architect, Inigo Jones.

Wren quickly remedied this *faux pas* with his next plan which, although he denied himself a central dome, allowed him two smaller ones. With these twin sentinels on either side, and a wide central gap, the Queen's House was not hidden.

Architecturally this was not an ideal solution because, as Canaletto's famous view (46) shows, the small house was dwarfed by the long vista and by the overbearing splendour of the new buildings.

The plan was accepted, however, and work began with the laying of the foundation stone by Wren and Evelyn, who was a commissioner of the Hospital. The time, exactly calculated by Flamsteed, the Astronomer Royal, was 5 p.m. on 30 June 1698.

Accommodation in the Hospital was to be for 2,000 seamen, and if they lacked the scarlet plumage of their Chelsea counterparts, their uniform of tailcoat, breeches and blue cocked hat was distinctive. Artists could rarely resist the temptation of showing them happily carousing with peg legs and single arms.

Forty-two disabled men were admitted when Greenwich Hospital opened in 1705. In the next thirty years numbers increased to 1,000 with an eventual total of 3,000. Their weekly rations consisted of seven 11 lb loaves, 3 lbs of beef and 2 lbs of mutton, peas, cheese and butter. They were also allowed fourteen quarts of beer and one shilling's worth of tobacco. Their clothing included an issue of two night caps.

The inmates were overshadowed by their setting. Wren's talents were combined with those of Vanbrugh and Hawksmoor to provide London with the greatest example of the grand baroque style. Wren's exact contribution is uncertain. He is thought to have started the King William block which contained the Painted Hall and the Queen Mary block with the Chapel. He was said to be determined to outdo Les Invalides, Mansart's domed hospital building in Paris. A suggestion by Hawksmoor that the Queen's House should be moved bodily back into the park with another storey added to make it more impressive is best forgotten.

The Painted Hall was the central masterpiece thanks largely to James Thornhill, England's first 'history painter'. He spent twenty years on the ceiling, an allegorical composition in which William and Mary recline in a bower under a white and gold canopy to symbolize the Triumph of Peace and Liberty. They are surrounded by 200 figures gambolling in various stages of undress to represent Vice, Virtue, Science

46. Canaletto's view of Greenwich, 1755.

and Art. A pensioner, aged ninety-eight, modelled the white-bearded character of Winter, and Thornhill himself modestly peers round a pillar in the Upper Hall mural (39).

The great domed and colonnaded buildings were to be a home for disabled and aged seamen for 180 years. The residents were inclined to be less enthusiastic than visitors about their surroundings. 'Columns, colonnades and friezes ill accord with bull beef and sour beer mixed with water', observed one crusty captain. Clearly he was not satisfied with his two pints a day. Old salts complained of the food, boredom and excessive stairs up which they had to drag their wounded limbs to the dormitories. They also resented being forced to wear their coats inside-out as a punishment for infringement of rules. But when he reached the lofty wards - each named after a ship - the pensioner had a bed and privacy in a small cabin of his own. The cabin was his exclusive possession and filled with any personal ornaments he fancied. Worse things, some may have reflected, happen at sea.

47. A Hospital pensioner acting as a guide in the Painted Hall, by Thomas Rowlandson.

48. Vanbrugh Castle (A. See map p.41).

VANBRUGH CASTLE

Architect, playwright and soldier, Sir John Vanbrugh succeeded Wren as Surveyor of Greenwich Hospital in 1716. He needed somewhere to live, and in the following year leased twelve acres of 'upland' on top of Maze Hill. While he was designing Blenheim Palace, the Duchess of Marlborough had prevented Vanbrugh from developing a medieval manor house in the grounds of Woodstock. Now this house, known as 'Rosamund's Manor', became the inspiration for his Greenwich home. For seventeen months an army of bricklayers, slaters, plumbers and carpenters toiled on the site. The result was a crenellated 'Gothick' folly called Vanbrugh Castle.

The architect is also thought to have modelled this fortress home on the Bastille in Paris where he was briefly imprisoned, and this notion is consistent with a letter to a friend, the Duke of Newcastle, who had called on him one day when he was out. Vanbrugh wrote: 'I hear your Grace was pleased to Storm my Castle yesterday. I hope next time you'll be so gallant to let me know your Design...when I'll endeavour to give you a Warmer Reception.'

Not content with one Gothic castle, Vanbrugh decided to build four more. The others have gone but their sites can be plotted on a modern map (p.41). The

49. Sir John Vanbrugh; engraving from a portrait by Sir Godfrey Kneller.

50. Vanbrugh House from the south c1830 (B).

approach to this collection of follies was by an arched Gateway (55) – straddling the modern road called Vanbrugh Fields – designed much in the style of his gates at Chatham Dockyard. Through the arch, the road led up to Vanbrugh House, massive with side turrets (50), which Sir John built for his son Charles in 1722. These strange buildings were very much a family affair. Flanking the drive from the gate was the White Tower first occupied by his brother Capt. Charles Vanbrugh, RN (51). Next to this was a long, low crenellated building named 'The Nunnery' (52), built for another brother Philip, also a naval officer, and where Sir John's widow eventually settled. South

51. White Tower c1905 (C).

52. The Nunnery c1911 (D).

53. Second White Tower c1905 (E).

of that was a second White Tower (53) – twin to the first - intended rather prematurely for a son who died in infancy.

Buildings in the Frankenstein manner beguiled the Victorians but stern twentieth-century realists had no time for creeper-clad pastiche. Vanbrugh House went first, demolished in 1903; the two White Towers were pulled down in 1905; the Gateway disappeared sometime after 1905; and in 1910 the Nunnery which had never known a holy sister was flattened.

This left only the castle. Its rambling outbuildings and winding corridors have been much altered over the years. They were sufficiently gloomy and oppressive to be considered suitable for a school for boys. The RAF then took the castle over as a memorial home, and in 1977 it was divided into four private residences. With turrets breaking the skyline, Vanbrugh Castle still astonishes the unprepared when they reach the top of Maze Hill.

55. Gateway c1905 (F).

54. Sites of Vanbrugh's follies.

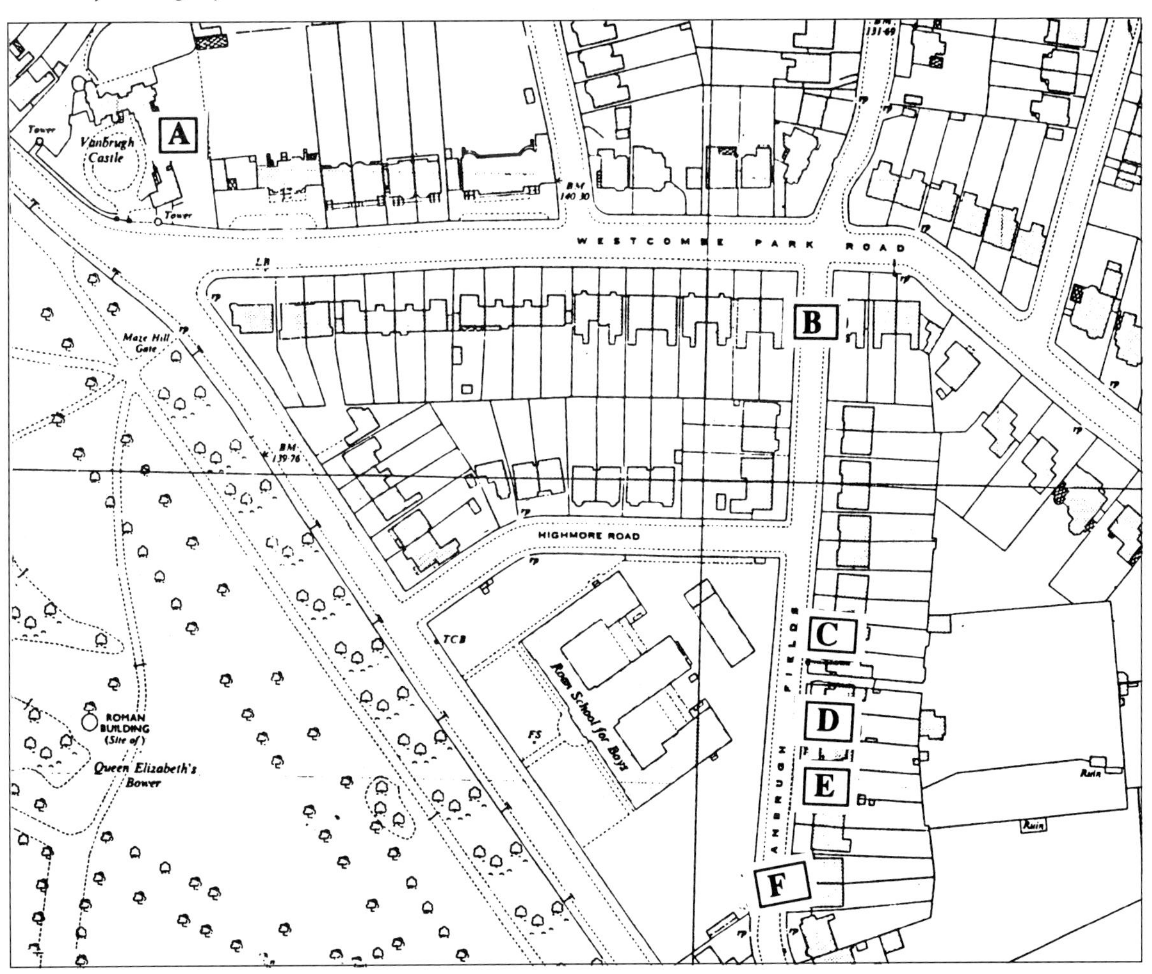

GREENWICH PARK

The story of Greenwich Park goes back 400 years – to 1433 when, with Parliament's assent, Henry VI granted his uncle Duke Humphrey 'licence to enclose two hundred acres of their land, pasture, wood, heath...and gorse thereof to make a park in Greenwich'. This enclosure of land, until then part of Blackheath, made it the first royal park to be created in London.

In early Tudor times the park retained the appearance of a wild heath although enclosed by a wooden fence. The first keeper was appointed in 1486. Deer were introduced from Rayleigh Park in Essex in 1520, and Henry VIII enjoyed the royal domain for hunting and hawking. Later, oaks and elms were to be felled for timber. In James I's reign the fencing was replaced by a two-mile brick wall, twelve feet high, much of which survives.

56. Map of Greenwich Park, 1749. From the London Magazine.

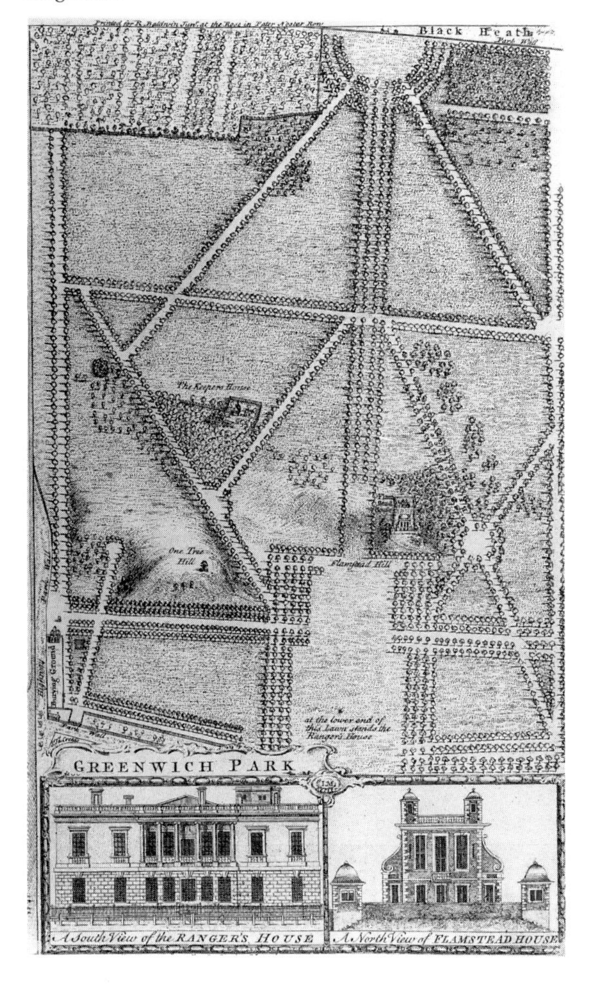

57. Early nineteenth-century holiday scene in Greenwich Park. George Arnold's sedate, idealistic scene contrasts with more boisterous 'gambols' shown by other artists.

During the Commonwealth there was a plan to end royal ownership of the park by selling it into private hands but this was abandoned because Cromwell, who preferred Greenwich to Whitehall, had an idea – never realized – of making it his home.

Soon after the Restoration Charles II decided that he wanted to improve the park. While in exile he had seen Versailles and admired the gardens created there and at the Chateau Vaux-le-Vicomte, near Fontainbleu, by Louis XIV's landscape gardener, André Le Nôtre. Charles wrote to the French King who gave permission for Le Nôtre to come to Greenwich. Whether he did or not is an unsolved mystery.

A treasury account of the period attributes Greenwich Park to Le Nôtre, and Hawksmoor writing later refers to 'The Regular Designs of that Most Admirable Person Monsieur Le Nôtre in Esplanades, Walks, Vistas, Plantations and lines of that beautiful Park'. But other evidence is conflicting.

Variations of Le Nôtre's proposal have survived. There are at least two redrawn versions of his comprehensive plan for the whole park, one of them

shown in (56). The other, (58), shows the grounds immediately south of the Queen's House and is annotated in the designer's own hand. Illustration (56), a more extensive map, shows the central avenue as it is today with a semi-circle of trees by Blackheath Gate from which other diagonal avenues splay out like spokes of a wheel. This map gives the impression that the designer envisaged a fine vista with the Queen's House at the far end. But a fall in the ground of over 150 feet would prevent any such vista and this has led to the belief that Le Nôtre could not have visited the site because he would never have perpetrated such a fundamental mistake.

However, yet another variation of Le Nôtre's overall plan shows a flight of large steps at the point where the land drops away. The central feature of this plan, annotated in Le Nôtre's own hand, shows a large circle as part of a formal garden. If this is a water basin, it confirms an idea in Charles's mind when he wrote a letter to France in 1664. 'Pray lett Le Nostre goe on with the model,' wrote the King, 'and only tell him this addition that I can bring water to the

58. Map of Greenwich Park annotated by André Le Nôtre

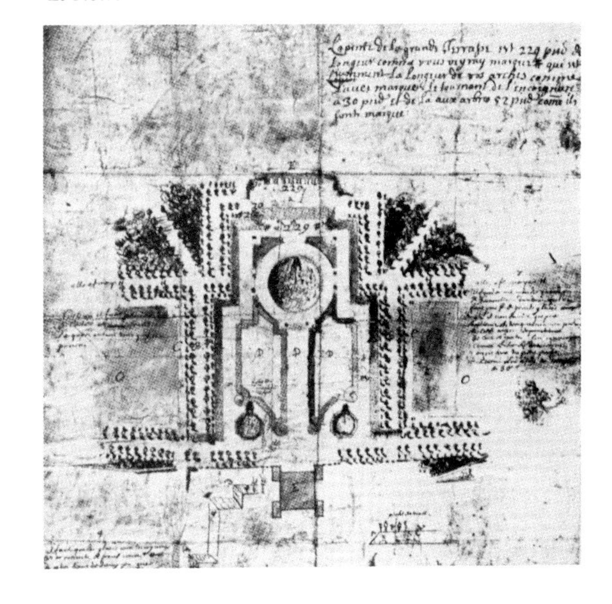

59. 'Holyday Gambols' on Greenwich Hill, c1750.

60. Tumbling on Observation Hill; detail from a print by George Cruikshank.

top of the hill, so that he may add much beauty of the descente by a cascade of watter.'

In other words Charles envisaged a formal garden for his mother's home on the pattern of Vaux-le-Vicomte with water pouring down 150 feet of steps. A waterfall would have been a magnificent feature, and would explain what Le Nôtre had in mind. The question of whether the French landscape designer actually came to this country is academic since Charles lost interest in Greenwich, halted work on the palace and never went ahead with the garden.

Further progress on Henrietta Maria's garden was stopped by Sir William Boreman, Keeper of the Park, when the Queen left in 1665 to return to France where she died four years later.

Aerial views of the modern park show several avenues (and traces of others) conforming to Le Nôtre's design, but instead of a long bubbling cascade we are left with a dull formal garden by the Queen's House. A rough, grassy slope replaced steps that have long since been worn away.

Slopes down from the Observatory were to have other uses in the eighteenth century when the public were first allowed into the park. As more people began to filter through the gates a pastime called 'tumbling' became popular. The *Daily Journal* for 4 April 1730 reported: 'On Tuesday last in Greenwich Park great numbers of people from London and the adjacent Parks diverted themselves, as is common on public Holidays, with running down the Hill (formally called the Giant's Steps) that fronts the Palace, but some others more venturesome would run down the steeper part of the said hill under the Terrace of the Royal Observatory.'

Tumbling had its dangers. The *Journal* reported a young woman breaking her neck, another her leg and a third her jawbone against a tree. But it remained popular for years and an 1820 diary describes how 'In rows the men and girls lined up across the Park and arm-in-arm ran down the slope: some kept their feet, some rolled to the bottom'.

Verses under a 1750 print of 'Holyday Gambols' advocate that 'sweet-scented Sirs [sick of] stale languid follies of the Ballroom or Court [could] For a change leave the Mall and to Greenwich resort'. Dr Johnson who lodged at Greenwich in his younger days wrote his poem *Irene* in the park. The exact whereabouts of his lodgings is uncertain. The doctor described them as being next to the Gold Hart in Church Street and the chances are that they were in one of a row of weatherboarded houses that existed until about 1900 on the west side.

Johnson would have pointed the house out to Boswell when they visited Greenwich half a century later in 1763 and landed at the Church Street steps. With customary enthusiasm Boswell made a production of the occasion. He took out a copy of Johnson's *London* poem and declaimed:

> 'On Thames's banks in silent thought we stood
> Where Greenwich smiles upon the silver flood:
> Pleas'd with the seat that gave Eliza birth
> We kneel and kiss the consecrated earth.'

He completed the performance by actually kneeling down and kissing the ground. Pausing only to make a characteristically sweeping criticism of Green-

61. Queen Elizabeth Oak, an ancient tree in the park, was surrounded in legends. The Queen is said to have danced round it with her father Henry VIII. Enveloped in ivy, the tree fell in heavy rain in the summer of 1991. It was replaced by a new oak planted by the Duke of Edinburgh the following year.

62. *Whit Sunday in Greenwich Park in 1835.*

wich Hospital ('too magnificent for a place of charity'), Johnson continued the sentimental pilgrimage by leading his friend into the park of which he had a better opinion. 'Is it not fine?', he demanded. For once his biographer was not cowed into acquiescence. His answer was either a *non sequitur*, or ironical. 'Yes,' he replied, 'but not equal to Fleet Street'.

For Greenwich residents the pleasant outlook praised by the doctor was threatened by the hordes from London who arrived for the fair in the town on bank holidays. A war against the invasion of the park was to be waged through mid-Victorian times but does not look very violent from the *Illustrated Times* of 1835 (62). This shows a few young people risking their necks, but the general scene lacks the wild abandon of a century earlier. Children play tag, pie-vendors wander through the crowd, women are given the eye by gallants, but the dominating figures are side-whiskered husbands in stove-pie hats with crinolined wives on their arms making a solemn show of concern as they listen to a pensioner's tall story.

63. *A panorama of Blackheath; 19th-century watercolour by an unknown artist.*

Enigmas of the Heath

Blackheath evades simple definition. From earliest times it has been an open space but, though it has acquired houses and sufficient shops to be called a village, Blackheath is not a parish or even a properly defined area. The Heath itself may be accepted as 270 acres acquired for London as an open space in 1871. But how many people can be described as living there is uncertain because the district, as such, is subject to no census.

For the compiler of gazetteers there is the further complication that Blackheath is partly in Greenwich and partly in Lewisham. Shooters Hill Road divides the boroughs but plenty of people north of the road consider they live on the Heath that they look out on. Others in the fringe areas of Kidbrooke and Lee regard themselves as being in Blackheath; so do those in the Greenwich hinterland of Westcombe Park; estate agents do not hesitate to include the area a quarter of a mile south of Belmont Hill, technically in Lewisham, as part of Blackheath.

It is probably best to ignore these confusions and

64. *Blackheath village in 1801. View from Whitefield's Mount (looking towards Royal Parade), shows West Mill in the left foreground with East Mill House behind. Surviving buildings from centre to right include Eastnor House, Grotes Place, the Hare and Billet and, behind the trees, Eliot Place.*

look at the Heath with the untroubled eye of artists in the past. Towards the end of the last century an unknown painter looking east towards the village presents an idyllic view. Sheep graze beside Hare and Billet Road. This is by a mistily outlined dip known as Marr's Ravine. In this tranquil period before traffic another artist, William Noble, in 1808 (64), provides a panorama with West Mill in the left foreground and a view stretching east towards the village. The buildings are a bit sketchy but this is the only chance to see Lamb's Buildings and Phoenix House which disappeared in 1861. Shooters Hill is in the far distance.

There were four Blackheath mills, one of them on Morden Hill, but only two windmills appear to have been operating at any one time – compared to seven on the Isle of Dogs – and the only explanation seems to be that in the valley below the Heath the Ravensbourne could offer more reliable water power. There were eleven watermills in Lewisham and four in Greenwich.

For an idea of the Heath's extent John Rocque's map (65) of 1746 is invaluable. The cartographer has marked a plateau called 'Blackheath Common' with hatching to define the falling away of land on the perimeter. As he shows, in the middle of the eighteenth century only a few isolated country mansions were dotted round the fringe of the Heath. There was no manor house, as at Charlton or Lee, to give focus to a village. The so-called Manor House, a fine building at the top of Crooms Hill just to the north of 'Genl Withers's Walk' on the map, is a misnomer. If any house has the right to the title it is the mansion of the earls of Dartmouth to the south-west. The first Earl's father acquired the status of Lord of the Manor at the end of the seventeenth century.

Another enigma – an unsolved mystery – is the Blackheath Triangle. On the maps of Rocque and Hasted for the last part of the eighteenth century the village is only roughly depicted, but when the next map appears in the following century a triangle of roads has appeared and their names are romantic. They are Montpelier Vale, Tranquil Vale and, rather later, Royal Parade. How they were given these

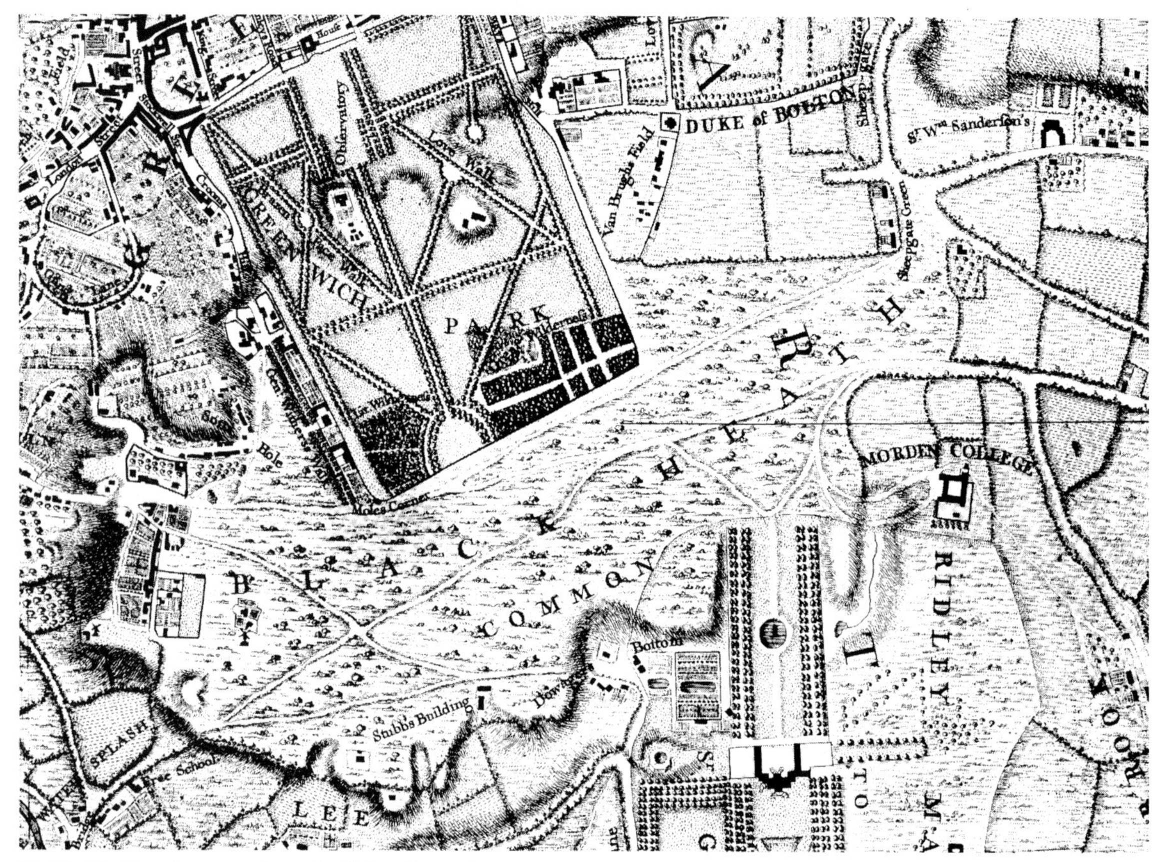

65. The Heath and surroundings, detail from Rocque's map.

names would be fascinating to know but unfortunately the rate books and parish records for the vital last thirty-four years of the eighteenth century have been destroyed. So the owners and early tenants of the two Vales as well as Montepelier Row remain unknown. There is no clue of who bestowed such lyrical names on them.

Blackheath is served today by five churches and one of them, All Saints (in the background of the idyllic view), which might seem to be the 'parish' church, has confident position but no ancient tradition. The Victorian building (87, p62) dates back only to 1857 and had for its architect a former pupil of Pugin.

The best view of London from Blackheath is from the top of Blackheath Hill, though not with rain and lightning crashing from a stormy sky (66). This is close to the Point, a chalk escarpment which has a mysterious cave under it. The Cavern (67), cut out of solid chalk to a depth of 160 feet, was discovered in 1780 and immediately excited wild surmise. Four large areas were connected by a passage and there was also a well for which there was no easy explanation.

The simplest solution was that it was an excavated 'chalk-pytte' of the fifteenth century, but popular imagination demanded something more romantic. The cavities became 'Dene holes' from which local inhabitants had hidden from the twelfth-century Viking invaders. How they would have survived below ground for two years is the kind of detail to which legend does not supply an answer.

Whatever the origin, the Cavern provided an excellent sideshow. From an entrance in Maidenstone Hill, visitors descended by 'Convenient Stepes' to 'Rooms perfectly dry, comfortable and lighted. Admission 6d'. A waxwork hermit was on show and a guide with lighted taper spun the story of 'Discords, horrid Murders and sanguinary Conflicts' between Saxons and early Britons. Jack Cade, at the head of 'disloyal, cruel and unprincipled Rebels' was dragged into the story and 'since then several Banditti, called Levellers in the Rebellious Commotion of Oliver Cromwell'. Stories spread of underground passages linking the Cavern with the Queen's House and even as far as Chislehurst Caves.

66. The Great Storm of 1846. From the Illustrated London News, *8 August.*

67. A view of the Cavern in the 1850s.

An entrepreneur, Mr J. Sleaman, organized a Grand Bal Masque in 1850 with a band and at a shilling a head people enjoyed music which, he claimed, sounded 'truly wonderful at 280 feet below the ground'. The depth was a showman's exaggeration. A second ball followed a month later and in 1853 a further masked ball was held which ended in panic when jokers extinguished all the lights. Confused revellers groped their way out, but after this incident the Cavern was firmly sealed. Unvisited, it survived in stories of unspeakable orgies and black magic until 1938, when there was an idea to make it into an air raid shelter. The idea was dropped, and the caves have remained closed save for an official inspection in 1946 when mementoes from the panic stricken ball of a century earlier were said to be found.

Except at two places, the Heath no longer shows the scars made by gravel pits from the seventeenth century. The pits and hollows were largely filled up with bomb damage rubble after World War II and smoothed out to provide a larger area for playing fields. But Blackheath gravel was of such good quality that Louis XIV offered Charles II paving stones in exchange for gravel he needed at Versailles - an arrangement that was not followed through. Ballast Quay on Greenwich waterfront derives its name from the cargoes brought down Maze Hill by horse and cart from the workings on the Heath.

One of the biggest pits was Marr's Ravine between Hare and Billet Road and Goffers Road, mistily discernible in the watercolour, which was not filled

68. Eliot Place on the north side of the Heath in 1852. Schools occupying some of the houses railed off part of the Heath for sports.

in until 1905. Another was Crown Pits by Greenwich Park (where the fair is now held), and Washerwomen's Pits, opposite the Royal Parade, were filled in with rubble after 1945. How the pits looked - but now covered in gorse - is seen opposite Vanbrugh Park (69). The 'Dips', now enjoyed for tobogganning on Mounts Pond Road, was also a former gravel pit. An even larger excavation resulted in the creation of Blackheath Vale in which a small community has a sunken existence in what looks like a volcanic crater off Goffers Road.

These semi-industrial activities are not what the turn-of-the-century camera is looking for when it searches out children paddling in the pond by Whitefield's Mount (70) and shows the 'Rotten Row' for horse riding to the left of Prince of Wales Road (71).

69. Old gravel pits by Vanbrugh Park.

70. *Children paddling at Whitefield's Mount.*

71. *Pond on Prince of Wales Road, early in the 20th century.*

THE VILLAGE EVOLVES

When John Rocque surveyed the south-east side of the Heath in the 1740s there was nothing to indicate a village. He simply marked six buildings at a place called 'Dowager's Bottom'. They were a public house (The Crown) and a few cottages (now part of Collins Square).

This was the embryonic Blackheath Village, and within sixty years it had consolidated with more than a hundred traders and small businesses into a triangle with Tranquil Vale and Montpelier Vale as the converging sides and, as its base, Royal Parade, soon to be built overlooking the Heath. The two 'Vales' joined to become a single road in a valley called Blunt's Hole (named after a long-forgotten Tudor landowner, Edward Blount of the Middle Temple). This road went into a dip through which the railway was soon to thrust and, at the top of a short steep rise, continued down to Lee and branched along Belmont Hill to Lewisham.

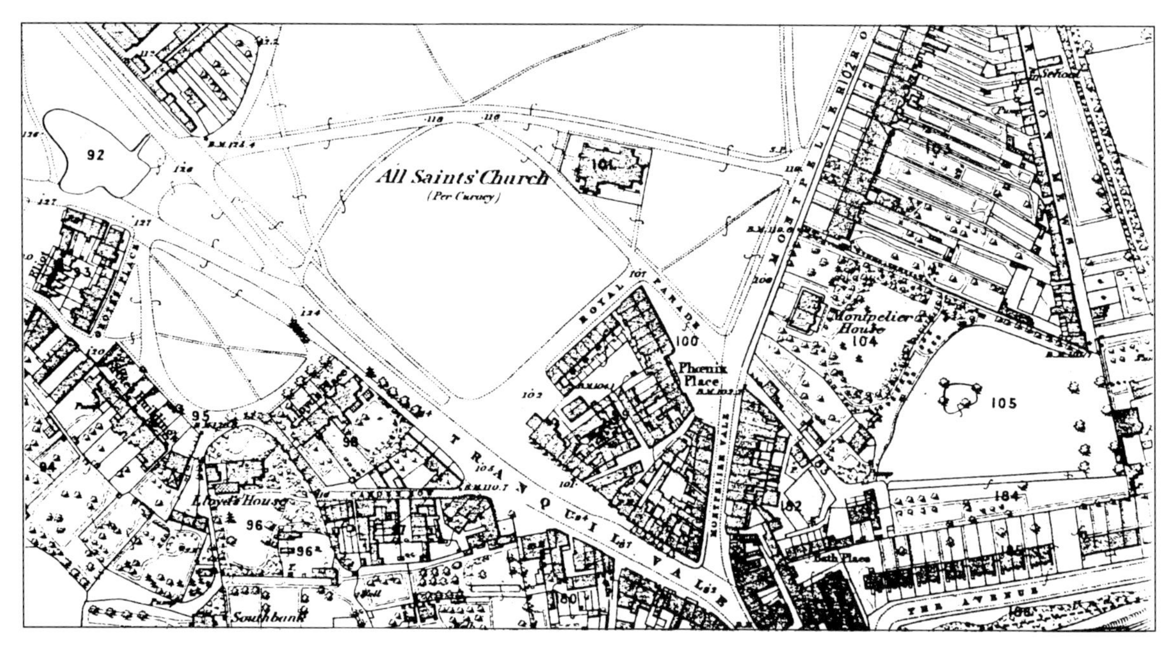

72. *Ordnance Survey map of Blackheath, 1863.*

73. *Hally's Nursery, Blackheath, 1852. Billhead.*

74. Vignette looking down Tranquil Vale.

Villages generally evolve round a green and communal pump. Blackheath grew round a public well (site in Tranquil Passage), the Crown inn and a house opposite which became an inn (the Three Tuns). Around the triangle shops appeared; a church shot up on the Heath; and rural peace ended with the arrival of the railway in 1849. By 1863 the Ordnance Survey (72) showed these buildings consolidated and spreading.

Two beguiling mid-century views show the apex of the triangle, one (74) looking down Tranquil Vale, the other (75) showing Tranquil Vale from the opposite direction. A business letterhead of 1852 (73) provides a delightful view of a flower shop (site of Barclays Bank on the corner of Blackheath Grove) and a nursery in the valley which cannot have liked the railway.

Mid-century Blackheath Village has evolved; now it is necessary to see how changes to two great estates brought this about.

75. Looking up Tranquil Vale, Tuck's Corner, early 1850s.

76. The portico of Morden College, showing the statues of the founders, Sir John and Lady Morden.

Great Blackheath Landlords and Estates

SIR JOHN MORDEN

The most important event in Blackheath's development as a village and residential suburb started with the purchase of an estate and the founding of a college by Sir John Morden in 1695. At almost exactly the same date another great landlord, Baron Dartmouth, purchased a manor with widespread holdings on the opposite side of the Heath. But it was Morden, a mile away to the east, whose acquisition was to have the greatest effect on the village itself.

Sir John's benefaction gains colour from the legendary story of how it came about. As a prosperous City merchant, Morden thought himself ruined but enjoyed a seemingly miraculous recovery. A deputy governor of the East India Company, he lost three ships on a trading mission and, so the tale goes, was reduced to earning his livelihood working for a tradesman. Then one day four years later he overheard some talk that three long-lost ships had been recovered. They were his. As a thanksgiving he decided to build an almshouse for poor 'decayed' Turkey merchants of the Company. And so the charity, greatly expanded, exists to this day.

Whether or not this was how the charity started, there were good precedents for the foundation of such 'colleges'. Morden was a treasurer of a building for poor clergymen's widows at Bromley, and there were some fifteen similar almshouses around London. For a rich man without children, this was a benign way to devote time and money.

As a merchant in 1669 Morden was doing sufficiently well to buy a large manorial property called Wricklemarsh from the Blount family of 'Blunt's Hole' (see p. 54). He set about building the College on the edge of his estate with entrance gates in modern Morden Road. Wricklemarsh, probably a Tudor building and his actual home, was later so thoroughly demolished that no one knows exactly where Sir John and his wife lived. In his *Tour Through Great Britain* Defoe describes it as 'a great house at the going off from the Heath, a little to the south of the Hospital' (i.e. the College). Morden's vineyard and orchard appear on a contemporary survey and a little topographical deduction places the house in modern Cresswell Park, in the village where the Roman Catholic presbytery occupies the site. In the background to the portrait of Lady Morden (80) there is a building which could be Wricklemarsh.

From their home, it was a short walk of less than a quarter of a mile to Great Stone Field where work on the almshouse started in 1695 and took a couple of years to finish. Because of its style and elegance Sir Christopher Wren has been named as the architect, but no documentary evidence has come to light. The less eminent but prolific master mason Edward Strong is thought to have carried out the work. He, like Wren, was engaged on Greenwich Hospital at the time and as Morden was a commissioner it would have been almost impossible for Wren not to have had at least an advisory hand in the design.

Well sited on the slope at the edge of the Heath, Morden College would certainly not disgrace Wren.

77. The quadrangle of Morden College; sketch by T. Frank Green, 1915.

Built in warm-coloured brick and decorated with stone quoins and cornices, it is very much in his manner. Round a cloister-like quadrangle were the rooms for the 'poor, decayed and ruined merchants', four of whom (out of a future forty) took up residence when the college opened in 1700. They also received a £20 pension 'so that they could live like gentlemen', but the numbers of inmates – like the size of the pension – was to fluctuate over the years. Two fountains played in the quadrangle and with a fine chapel (carving inevitably attributed to Grinling Gibbons), Morden College deserved the understated description in Strype's Stow of 'a very fair and spacious structure'.

Eight years after the opening Sir John died and overseeing was carried on by his wife Susannah who survived him by thirteen years. Living so near the College both had shared a close interest in shaping the rules, seeing they were observed and ensuring the pensioners' welfare. In the rules Lady Morden was named as 'Foundress'. In widowhood she became the dowager (of 'Dowager's Bottom', named in Rocque) and in her will she arranged for stone effigies of herself and her husband to be carved and erected over the entrance (76). The two benefactors were buried in the College chapel.

79. Sir John Morden.

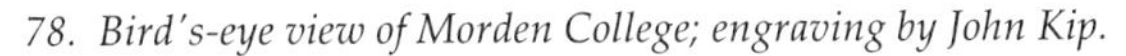

78. Bird's-eye view of Morden College; engraving by John Kip.

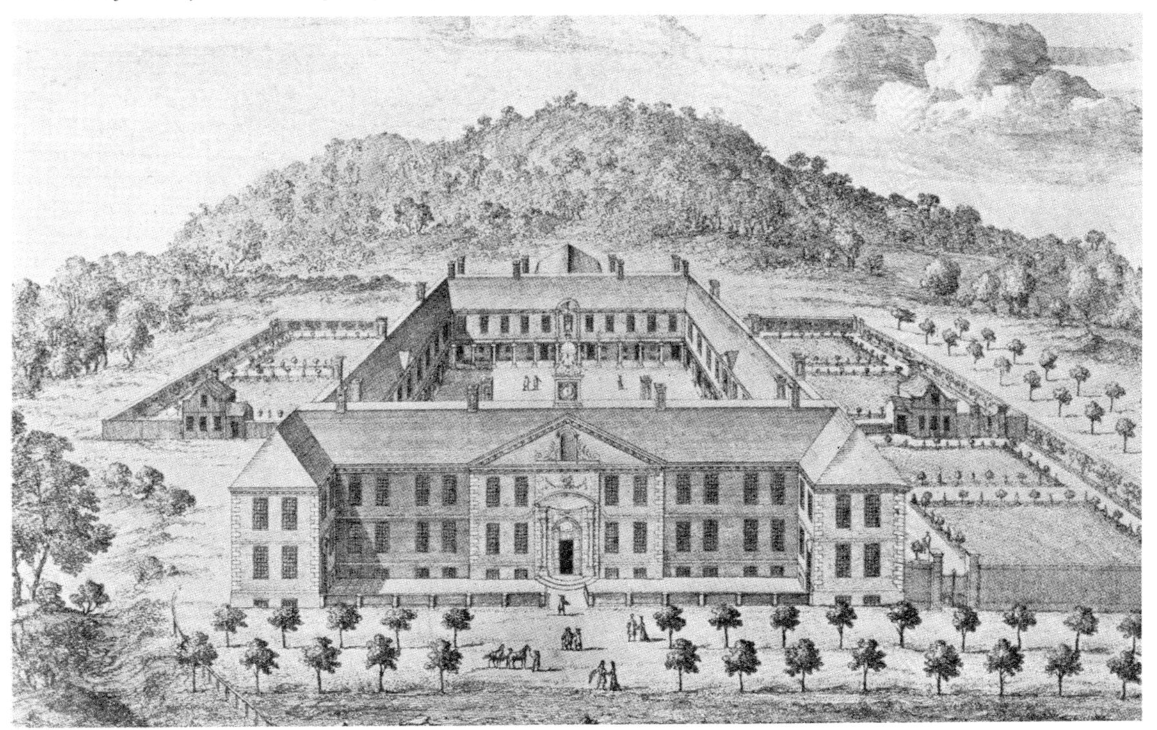

80. Lady Morden with possibly Tudor Wricklemarsh in the background.

SIR GREGORY PAGE

Two years after the death of Dame Susannah Morden Wricklemarsh was sold to the immensely rich Sir Gregory Page who had made a fortune out of the South Sea Company and then lived in a fine house in the north-east corner of Greenwich Park.

Page acquired the twenty-two acre park and 271 acres of agricultural land for £9,000. He had spectacular plans for a new house on which he started work in 1723. He had no use for Morden's Tudor Wricklemarsh and so obliterated it completely. Departing from the style of his previous William and Mary house in Greenwich, he went for the increasingly popular Georgian style.

The new Wricklemarsh was built within a year, a magnificent mansion (81) and a fitting home in which to entertain King George II and to display a collection of paintings that included a Rubens, Van Dyck and Titian. Once again Rocque provides a valuable record with his detailed map showing the position of Page's mansion. The house was perfectly placed on a high ridge (present Blackheath Park, where St Michael's Church is today). The Ionic portico commanded a fine view to the south and east overlooking Shooters Hill, Eltham and a part of Kent. To the north Page faced the Heath with the Thames beyond. His southern boundary was modern Eltham Road..

Page chose a comparatively unknown local man, John James, as his architect. It is hard to imagine why. As the richest commoner in England he could have beckoned such great figures of the day as William Kent, Lord Burlington or James Gibbs. Instead he engaged the middle-aged James, formerly a carpenter and surveyor, whose recent work had been to add the steeple to St Alphege's, Greenwich. Like many dilettantes of the day, Page may have fancied himself as a designer and merely wanted a draughtsman who would follow his instructions.

Wricklemarsh was completed in eleven months, so quickly that Page was openly accused of using stone and materials that were intended for Greenwich Hospital where work was suspended for a year. The result was 'a house of masterly paintings, rich hangings, marbles and altonelievos [high relief decoration]...to command the attention of every person in geniius and taste' (Thomas Fisher's *Kentish Travellers Companion*, 1771). Laid out with avenues of chestnuts and plane trees, Page's park appears on some maps even larger than the royal one at Greenwich. Unlike the Mordens who had let cottages and much of their large estate, Page knocked down smaller dwellings and enclosed as much as he could for grandiose effect. He tried unsuccessfully to

81. Eighteenth-century Wricklemarsh, the home of Sir Gregory Page. By W. Watts, 1782.

divert a stream from the Heath, perhaps to create a lake, but had instead two artificial ponds at the front and back of his house. One is still delineated by the circle in Pond Road, the other, Lay Pond to the south, is fed by branches of the Kid Brook.

Pepys wrote admiringly of Page's life of 'great splendour and hospitality' with a 'princely magnificence' comparable to the Medicis. But Lord Egmont, writing his diary in Charlton House nearby, strikes a different note with an account of two attempted suicides by Page, of the unwarranted jealousy of his wife and how 'being alone he knew no way to amuse himself but by walking from one room to another...'.

Page's reign of glory lasted fifty years. He moved into his Palladian palace when he was thirty-four and died there, a widower, in 1775. He was buried alongside his wife at St Alphege's. Like the Mordens, he and his wife Lady Martha had no children and the estate went to his great nephew, Gregory Turner, who added Page to his name to qualify for the inheritance. After a few attempts to tenant the house – he had no taste for so unwieldly a home – Page-Turner put the house up for auction in 1783. Wricklemarsh (on which Sir Gregory had spent perhaps as much as £120,000) and the estate were sold to John Cator Esq., of Beckenham Place, Stumps Hill, Beckenham.

82. Sir Gregory Page

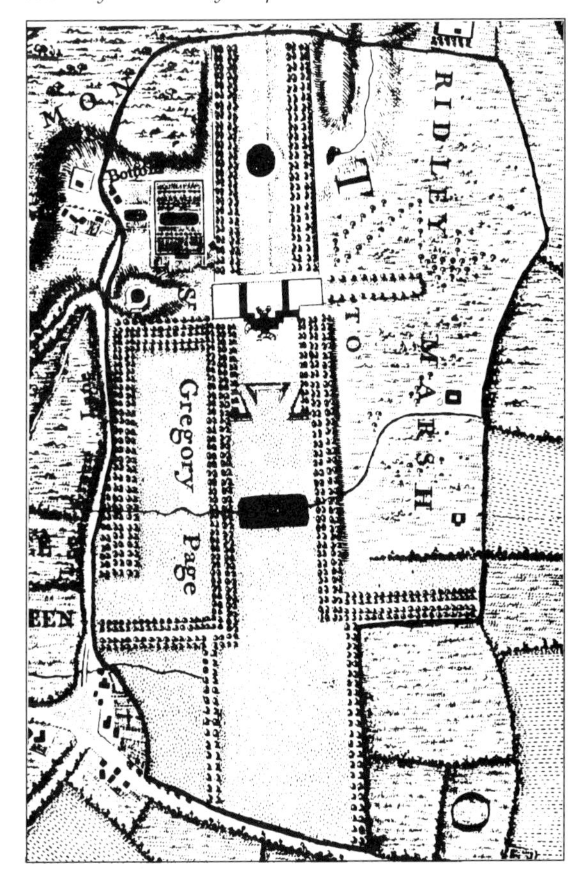

83. Extent of Page's estate, assumed to be the surrounding boundary delineated by Rocque.

THE EARLS OF DARTMOUTH

The way a family flourishes by slowly developing property on the edge of common land can be complicated. The process is often hard to unravel because stealthy encroachment was unlikely to be challenged provided parish dues were paid. An example, hardly to be bettered, is seen with the acquisition of land and the building of property on Blackheath by the Legge family – future earls of Dartmouth – and dates back to 1673 when George Legge became Lord of the Manor of Lewisham. This was a titular position that came to him through his aunt. Nine years later he was created Baron Dartmouth and the year after that he was granted the right to hold fairs on the Heath and drew the revenues that went with them. Like his title, this licence for a fair would have been some small reward from Charles II for Legge's services as an admiral and army commander.

Having put down his roots in the area, George Legge and his aunt Susanna granted building licences for eleven houses in a road named after him – Dartmouth Row – and these included the Green Man public house. To do so he nibbled away the

85. George Legge, 1st Baron Dartmouth (1648-91), by Sir Peter Lely.

84. Spencer Perceval House.

86. Dartmouth House.

fringe of the Heath and started a programme of building encroachment. Coinciding with the time that John Morden of Wricklemarsh was planning Morden College across the Heath, the Dartmouths were extending their interests on the west. Dartmouth Hill, Dartmouth Grove and Dartmouth Terrace were further extensions of hegemony.

Building made possible by this encroachment began in 1691 and included Dartmouth House (86), occupied by George Legge's son William, first Earl of Dartmouth. An even more stately house was a two-storey, nine-bay mansion later known as Spencer Perceval House (84) almost next door. As on the Dartmouths' Westminster property in Queen Anne's Gate, lively keystone faces over the windows were distinguishing features.

The Dartmouth Estate was not confined to the west side of the Heath. In the triangle at the centre of Blackheath Village the so-called Queen Elizabeth's Well in Tranquil Passage was Dartmouth property and so was the Three Tuns public house. A tell-tale clue is a narrow alley named Dartmouth Passage. Other Dartmouth holdings became lost with time because of leasing and sub-leasing. The garden of the Three Tuns was Dartmouth land but forgotten for sixty-one years on a 2s. 6d. annual rent. Only when a collection of wooden dwellings in Camden Row, beyond the Crown public house, came to be rebuilt in the 1890s was it discovered that long-forgotten Dartmouth ground leases had to expire before work could start on the present small Victorian villas.

To what extent some of these encroachments were illegal is hard to say. The way they came about seems to have at least technical legality under a system whereby applicants wanting land applied to courts held by the Lord of the Manor and since the Dartmouths *were* the Lords of the Manor there was unlikely to be much opposition. Token compensation for infringements and the loss of public amenities would be made to parishes which thought themselves lucky to be paid money for some intractable piece of land whose ownership was ill defined. Dartmouth House, the first Earl's home and where he died in 1750, stayed in the family from the 1690s to about 1810, and near to it a pattern of Dartmouth interests is clearly marked. Between the house and Spencer Perceval House stands the Church of the Ascension and, consistent with family concern, it is on the site of an earlier chapel built by the seventeenth-century aunt Susanna. Before this, the Dartmouth name was established after a stall erected for the fairs became a permanent structure known as the Market House. This in turn became the Duke's Head public house, doubling as the district's first official post office after 1752. The post office moved across the road to 18 Dartmouth Row in 1836 and combined with a little general shop remained open until 1979. It is now a private house.

ENCROACHMENTS

The backs of houses in Eliot Place define the southern edge of the Heath with their long gardens showing the natural falling away of the land. They may be taken as the Heath's limit. But jutting out across the land is a large rectangle called the Orchard. Until 1780 this was part of the Heath but was acquired by a man who turned it into an orchard. In 1801 his encroachment was extended by the Earl of Dartmouth who rebuilt or converted an existing mansion which for the next half-century was occupied mostly by the widows and unmarried daughters of the earls of Dartmouth.

The house was converted into flats in 1921 and demolished in 1965 when it was replaced by a modern block, Lyncourt. One turn-of-the-century house was knocked down to build modern flats with vertical glazing. The creation of an architect, a playwright, a solicitor and four other rebels against conventional architecture, North Several was condemned by the conservationist Blackheath Society as 'a disgusting building'.

Yet another encroachment was the building of a parish church for Blackheath in 1857. Several sites were considered before a curiously isolated position was chosen opposite Royal Parade. In the foreground of All Saints (87) is a dip caused by a gravel pit, now filled in, which was formerly known as Washerwomen's Bottom. A highly visible infringement, the church defied criticism because its sponsor, the fifth Earl of Dartmouth, laid the foundation stone and demonstrated practical piety by donating liberally to the cost.

A less obvious encroachment is the most extraordinary cluster of buildings on the Heath. Blackheath Vale consists of twenty-four houses and a small school all sunk in what seems to be a large volcanic crater. This was originally a huge sandpit – the largest on the Heath – and was leased by the third Earl of Dartmouth before being acquired by the Crown in the 1800s. There was a school here by 1830 where daughters of working people learned skills such as cookery, dressmaking and housework. Some seventy years later this strange cavity was occupied by a brewery, a livery stables and by another girls' school. There has been a stone mason's yard here for 150 years, and there remains a small community of troglodyte residents.

That encroachment of the Heath is not a danger that belongs to the far distant past is shown by the meeting (advertised by the poster, right) in which the defence of Blackheath – 'the People's Recreation Ground' – was the subject of an open meeting in 1870. A year later the Heath was adopted by the Metropolitan Board of Works which became responsible for the prevention of encroachments.

87. All Saints church, an ecclesiastical encroachment of the Heath..

DOES BLACKHEATH BELONG TO THE PEOPLE?

AN OPEN-AIR

MEETING

WILL BE HELD ON

Blackheath

On Saturday Evening next,

MAY 28th, 1870,

Under the auspices of the BORO' OF GREENWICH ADVANCED LIBERAL ASSOCIATION,

To consider the proposed Encroachments & Enclosure of the People's Recreation Ground—Blackheath.

J. BAXTER LANGLEY, Esq.,

LL.D., M.R.C.S., F.L.S.,

W.C.BENNETT, Esq.,

LL.D. And other Gentlemen will attend.

The Members of the Borough and County have been invited. Chair taken at half-past 6.

E. G. Berryman, Machine Printer, Bath House, Blackheath Road.

88. Poster advertising an open-air meeting in 1870 against encroachment on Blackheath.

JOHN CATOR'S TRANSFORMATION

In 1783 when John Cator, a wealthy Beckenham merchant who made his fortune in timber, bought Wricklemarsh for the bargain price of £22,550, Blackheath was on the verge of a transformation. The little village in the valley was about to spread. Roads and houses were soon to appear on the parkland which had been laid out by Sir Gregory Page. A garden suburb evolved but without the deadening uniformity the term often implies. Because of its period - Georgian into Regency becoming early Victorian - the houses were to have individuality, and the roads - Blackheath Park, Pond Road, Morden Road and Foxes Dale - a rural charm.

After the purchase of Wricklemarsh things did not happen in a hurry. A man of wide interests, Cator was a MP, Sheriff of Kent, a friend of Dr Johnson and of the Thrales. His widespread land investments in south London extended as far as Sydenham. With a splendid mansion, Beckenham Place, he had no wish to move to Wricklemarsh House. He was quite content to dismantle Page's palace and sell off the contents for £14,000. He transported the portico to Beckenham; fireplaces went to the Banqueting House in Whitehall; for a while he granted only a few building plots alongside the growing village.

The earliest recorded house to be built was on ground Cator leased to Capt. Thomas Larkins with the right to build a house on the west-facing slope of the village. This may well have been on the site of the long-lost home of Sir John and Lady Morden, whose whereabouts, possibly in Cresswell Park in the village, teases local historians.

90. John Cator; portrait by Sir Joshua Reynolds.

When John Cator died in 1806, Wricklemarsh Park was still mainly agricultural and the house only partly demolished. A guidebook of 1790 noted nostalgically: 'The seat of Sir Gregory Page, now pulling down, is at the south east extremity

89. Houses in Blackheath Park built in 1824 as part of the Cator Estate.

91. The Ordnance Survey of 1860 shows the extent of the Cator Estate with Blackheath Park the main west-east road.

92. Brooklands, c.1885.

of Blackheath...The house has been stripped of its interior beauties; and what was some years since a mansion fit for kings, now appears to the eye of the traveller a mass of ruins...'. The phrase 'now pulling down' is the guidebook's way of avoiding being out of date and the disappearance of the house does not appear to have taken place for several years.

In the year of Cator's death there is record of a plot being leased on 'the road to the ruins' (presumably reference to Wricklemarsh). This is now Blackheath Park, the proud east-to-west main artery from which stem other attractive roads graced by much sought-after houses. Of the same date – 1806 – was the Hall, one of the Cator Estate's great houses. Set in six acres of park and lived in by several distinguished tenants, it was pulled down in 1961 (p. 139) through a modern developer's conspiracy of neglect.

After 1819 the pace of development slightly increased and by 1824 the first four houses went up as separate buildings. These were to be altered to achieve today's terraced uniformity next to the church (89); they are now 31-43 Blackheath Park, and possess the Regency charm that so distinguishes much of the road. With steps leading up to proud porticos, several dignified Cator homes still survive. The architectural historian can enjoy seeing how old houses – among them, the Priory, Priory Lodge, Park Lodge, Falsgrave House – have been divided and converted but still remain monuments of gracious nineteenth-century living.

To the north, Pond Road stretched to the Heath and the limits of Cator's estate. Cator leased the land on the northern edge of his property in 1793 specifically for building development. His choice of lessee was a happy one for here a Southwark architect and surveyor Michael Searles was to create one of the gems of south-east London – the Paragon.

RURAL BLACKHEATH PARK

While land to the north of Blackheath Park was amply developed with houses, the gently sloping acres to the south remained for a long time in the hands of a few people. Only four small estates with large family homes stood in what were once known as pleasure gardens. These were well stocked with trees inherited by John Cator from the old Page estate and some enjoyed lakes and ponds supplied by the Kid Brook.

The most impressive house, which still survives on the Cator Estate, is Brooklands. Built in 1827, it stood in two acres of garden and had a further sixteen acres to the south. In a way it was a kind of mini Wricklemarsh and a photograph of 1885 (92) shows that in the grounds was a lake, a large sheet of ornamental water created in the previous century by John James, Sir Gregory Page's architect. Today houses have been built in this rural scene where the hay cart stands; there is the Blackheath and Greenwich Bowling Green to the south of the house; and Brooklands itself has been converted into five flats. Behind the trees to the right is Brooklands Park Road and beyond that, in the Casterbridge area, 289 London Council Council flats and Brooklands Primary School were built in the 1950s.

93. Blackheath Park with St Michael's church and one of the gas lamps that caused controversy.

George Smith, architect and original owner, would find Brooklands House not unduly changed from the time he built the house. Fellow of the Royal Institute of British Architects, Smith decided to live where he worked. The son of a local architect and surveyor to Morden College, he was the designer of the first London Bridge Station in 1843 and the natural person to get out plans for the Blackheath and Greenwich railway stations for which he is generally credited. Several buildings in Blackheath village were attributed to him, among them the Blackheath Literary Institution (p. 103), an elegant building with tall windows where reading room peace was disturbed by the railway.

'THE NEEDLE OF KENT'

Smith's most conspicuous monument, St Michael's (93), rose with its tall spire on the site of Page's Wricklemarsh House. Accepting the style of the period – one of the Cator family laid the foundation stone in 1828 – Smith had to forget his Italianate preferences in favour of ecclesiastical Gothic. The church was curiously orientated with the slim spire, known as the 'needle of Kent', at the east end. The contractor, it was said, misread the plans. Since George Smith was living only a stone's throw away, this is unlikely.

Though he always has an ear for a good story, Neil Rhind, Blackheath's historian, throws cold water on the legend that Smith, driven to frenzy by the mistake, climbed to the top of the steeple and threw himself off. The architect (Rhind notes, almost regretfully) died at Copthorne in Sussex in 1869 – and did so in his bed.

94. Satirical leaflet about gas installation in 1850.

Who Objects to Gas
IN
BLACKHEATH PARK?

Here's a pretty go! Here's impudence! Our wested interests, privileges and rights are threttened with inwashun.

Who Objecks indeed? We Objecks.

I objeck, cos Jeames cums a koorting of me in the dark, vich he coolld not doo vos gass a flaring at the Harey.

POLLY SLUTTERN, ***Housemaid.***

2nd. I objecks, cos Pliceman X, my betrothed, as young Miss says, likes the dark, and can get his witties and other things [illegible], without being stared at by Missuses prying eyes, vich so can my sister and her blessed children get a bundle now and then, vich as knowbody no's knowbody's [illegible].

SALLY SUET, ***Cook.***

3rd. I object. Once permit the gaseous fluid to introduce its impertinent ray, illuminating the innermost recesses of the garden, how could I procure that aliment necessary for the sustentation of the life and loveliness of my dear little ones, which now I do, by occasionally pruning the superfluous branches of rare plants, or by picking up stray bulbs, which otherwise would be left to rot in the

95. Queen Caroline.

96. The Pagoda.

QUEEN CAROLINE'S HIDEAWAY

Hemmed in by trees and modern houses, the Pagoda now attracts attention only because of old gossip and an oriental roof. The roof is a reminder of chinoiserie, a fashionable style in the middle of the eighteenth century when the Pagoda was built to serve as a summer house and sporting pavilion. This was an outpost of Montague House just across the heath, home of Caroline of Brunswick, the repudiated wife of the future George IV.

The Pagoda in Eliot Vale acquired spurious infamy after 1799 when Caroline of Brunswick began visiting this rustic pleasure house to tend a flourishing garden of flowers and vegetables. As she was lonely and denied the company of her daughter, Charlotte, she also ran a nursery school there. This sounds harmless, but it coincided with her husband's determination to get rid of her. In 1806 he instigated a Royal Commission hoping to prove allegations of immorality. Sir Thomas Lawrence, who painted her portrait (and once stayed overnight at Montague House), was one of several men accused of 'guilty intercourse' with her.

Caroline's enemies chose to regard the Pagoda nursery as a hideaway where she secretly housed one, if not two, illegitimate children. Testimony about Caroline's rowdy parties and kisses from admirers were true and servants produced damaging statements about visits by officers from the Royal Naval Hospital and alleged immoral comings and goings at all hours of the night. One officer was observed kissing her. The Commission, however, threw out a 20,000-word deposition from a neighbour that in 1802 she 'appeared to be with child'. They dismissed other stories of alleged bastards.

With its foreign appearance the Pagoda could be sure to excite gossip, and Caroline's subsequent behaviour lent fuel to the scandal. But her indiscretions were not in Blackheath but abroad and in Bayswater, where once she inadvisedly wandered about asking if there was anywhere she could rent for her nine children.

The Prince Regent never got his divorce, but Caroline was barred from the Coronation in 1821 and she died three weeks later. Napoleon's death that same summer seems to have led to confusion in George IV's mind. Told by a courtier that his greatest enemy was dead he exclaimed: 'Is she, by God!'

In 1815, the Prince Regent, as he still was, demolished Montague House (97), seemingly as a vindictive act against a woman he had so disliked. Only part of a wall and what looks like a sunken bath survives on the south-west corner of Greenwich Park.

A quarter of a mile away, the Pagoda has had a reverend member of the Dartmouth family as a tenant – he called it Chinese Cottage – and in the 1950s it escaped demolition as part of a LCC housing scheme. Now a local authority has returned the building to the use Caroline once put it – a children's home. It does not look unduly sinful.

97. *Montague House on the corner of Chesterfield Walk, described as 'a picturesque building of crenellated style' before its 1815 demolition. Drawing by Paul Sandby.*

CHESTERFIELD HOUSE

Since Montague House has been demolished, pride of place among the three important eighteenth-century houses fringing the west side of Greenwich Park has gone to Chesterfield House. This building with a fine facade – now known as Rangers House because it was long the 'grace and favour' residence of the park's ranger and nominal custodian – was occupied from 1748-73 by the fourth Earl of Chesterfield, diplomat and politician.

From here he wrote about 200 of his famous letters to his natural son. Published in 1774, and putting emphasis on manners and surface appearances, these homilies enjoyed some fame as a moral guide for adolescents.

Of his last seven years at the house Chesterfield wrote: 'Blackheath and a quiet conscience are the only objects of my cares. My little garden, the park, reading and writing kill time here tolerably...'

A few yards further down Chesterfield Walk is Macartney House. This third Georgian building is of importance because it was owned by the Wolfe family. General James Wolfe lived there between campaigns after 1751. Eight years later he said his goodbye to the house when he sailed for Quebec and his death. His embalmed body was brought back and lay in state in Macartney House.

98. *Chesterfield House, home of the Duke of Brunswick, as it looked in 1808.*

99. The Paragon

THE PARAGON

The year when Blackheath achieved the status of a fashionable and elegant place to live can confidently be dated. It was 1800 which saw the completion of the first stages of a crescent-shaped building called the Paragon. The dictionary definition of a paragon as 'a model of supreme excellence' was a fair description of the classical design.

In that year – 1800 – the first two houses were ready for occupation out of a final total of fourteen that would eventually be linked by a series of Tuscan colonnades.

It must have been an even more striking feature standing in isolation on open agricultural land than it is today. But there was at least one precedent for this style of crescent-shaped terrace. Michael Searles, the architect, had created a previous Paragon in the New Kent Road a few years before. He built this Southwark Paragon (demolished 1898) for the Rolls Estate and he himself lived there for three years.

During construction Searles was able to oversee the work from No. 14, at one end of the crescent. He started building from the centre to the ends. His first proposal had a central block with a full dress portico and an imposing pediment as its main feature (101). This he modified using taller buildings linked by colonnades (102 and 103).

Searles may not have had any intimations of the immortality the Paragon was to win him. Trained as a surveyor in informal partnership with his father who was a carpenter and craftsman, he was a practical builder but had a streak of imagination to create the unusual. Among more mundane building work in Bermondsey and Kennington, he managed to conceive pleasing Georgian designs.

John Cator, whose Palladian home, Beckenham Place, showed his classical taste, saw that Searles was the man to lend prestige with a similar style of architecture on the edge of the Heath. It must have been an even more striking feature in isolation on his agricultural land than it is today.

The time was ripe for Blackheath to join Hampstead, Richmond and Dulwich as a place to attract well-to-do professional and middle-class families who wanted to enjoy the air of the Heath. 'The

100. *Vignette of the Paragon, 1852.*

neighbourhood is of the first respectability and the distance from town easy' went the smooth rubric of the estate agent, possibly anxious to quell alarming stories of highwaymen and robberies on the Heath.

'Capital Family Residence with nine acres of land, Paragon, Blackheath' read an advertisement in *The Times* in 1801 which assured anyone purchasing the lease that No. 1 the Paragon was 'replete with every convenience for use, comfort and elegance' and was 'abounding with pleasant views in every direction!' The house offered two handsome drawing rooms, eight family bedrooms, a library and boudoirs, dressing rooms and 'gentleman's room' (for smoking, it is presumed). There was an ample cellar, a dairy, and a coachhouse. Bow windows looked out over long gardens at the back.

Searles had a difficult time when there was a slump as a result of the 1793 war with France. The last houses (Nos 9 and 10) were not finished until 1806 but from then on - and for the next 150 years until it was eventually broken up into 100 flats - the Paragon attracted the residents for whom it was planned. Ratebooks reveal rich bankers, lawyers, shipowners, City merchants, architects, surgeons, ministers, a bishop of Woolwich and a past lord mayor of London. Among others were the headmaster of Blackheath Proprietary School, an art historian, a royal academician and Sir John Simon, London's first officer of health.

After the First World War there were hints of a slight falling off of social standards. There were frowns in the 1920s when an hotel - even though it was a private one - opened at No. 6 and No. 9. The Paragon's Schools of Equitation and Ballroom Dancing were curious arrivals at No. 7 in the 1940s. At the end of the First World War Blackheath Girls' School had a house for boarders. But the Paragon's reputation was most seriously affected by two arrivals in its earliest days.

101. *Searles's ambitious drawing for a proposed centre block in the high classical manner was never carried out.*

102. *His second version of the Paragon with an extra storey added, side colonnades linking the individual houses and decorated pediment with shell motif.*

103. *Searles's drawing of the final version with an attic storey with dormer windows and no pediment.*

TWO DUBIOUS LADIES

Scaffolding was still up at No. 3 the Paragon when, as the account book records (104), Charlotte Sharpe, aged 27, and Eliza Robertson, who was 24, arrived in 1800. These two teachers who had run a small school together on Crooms Hill immediately began to spend wildly and lavishly. They managed to take the lease without a deposit and decorated extravagently, always demanding credit. They squandered £1,000 on beds and mattresses alone. One mirror cost £1,500.

A footman was engaged. They bought an earl's coach emblazoned with coronets that impressed shopkeepers on their spending sprees. Eliza put it around that she was due to marry a rich colonel, a plan rather discounted by her preference for men's clothing. The pair were denounced by the local Methodist minister as lesbians and when a Greenwich paper openly described them as 'the Swindlers of Blackheath' the time had come for flight. By this time Blackheath shops had extended huge credit. An ironmonger was owed £485, a glazier £567 and a carpenter who had built them an aviary and garden furniture wanted their arrest for a debt of £1,193. They fled leaving behind bills for £20,000.

The law landed Eliza in the Fleet Prison where, sometimes visited by Charlotte, she died in 1805 aged 32. Hastily the Paragon set about repairing its somewhat tarnished image.

105. Eliza Robertson.

104. Extract from the local rate books detailing the residence of the Misses Sharp and Robertson.

William Reeves for Coachhouses & Stables } 9 10 — 12 8 — 9¾ „ 13 5½ „ „ „

Paragon, Blackheath.

90 William Thompson for a House, Lodge House, Coach houses & Stabling } 88 — 57¼ — 74 6 4 8 „ „ „

a 91 Thomas Barnard 64 — 45¼ — 54 4 10 8 „ „ —

E 92 Misses Sharp & Robertson } 72 — 46 — 6 — „ „ „ 5 2 0

£ 2640 1129 22 4 10 . 5 11 11

106. Gloucester Circus.

GLOUCESTER CIRCUS

While the Paragon was taking slow but successful shape on Blackheath, Michael Searles still had to contend with the financial problems of a slightly earlier project in Greenwich. After the completion in 1790 of his lesser Paragon in the New Kent Road, he had gone on to a big challenge, his first large speculative venture – a circus lying between Crooms Hill and Royal Hill.

At the age of forty he must have seen Gloucester Circus as his big chance to shake off the lingering description of 'surveyor' and emerge as an architect and builder in his own right. Now his plan for a double crescent – Gloucester Circus – offered scope for his talents, and personal investment in a consortium would let him reap proper rewards.

A map of 1834 (110) shows the crescent in virtual isolation on a hillside dropping down from the Heath. Before the north side was built and with only a few houses dotted in surrounding fields, front windows on the crescent had views of the river.

The site was on three acres that had previously been a school called Greenwich Academy, and on his retirement as headmaster in 1788 the Revd A. James formed a consortium to exploit the land. The idea was a circus – an elongated oval in shape – through which a road would run for 150 yards between Crooms Hill and Royal Hill.

The consortium was an unusual combination of talents: James, ground landlord; Searles, architect and builder; a carpenter; a glazier, a plumber, a Bermondsey bricklayer and two blacksmiths. The intention was to build the north crescent as soon as the south one was finished but the plan hit snags which also affected the Paragon. The French war created a loss of financial confidence.

Searles, whose personal money was invested, faced bankruptcy two years later but he managed to survive. Construction began at the Crooms Hill end where an entrance was cut through to the road. Twelve houses were completed and occupied before the slump. After this building went on only slowly with the last two of the twenty-two houses not finished until 1809 – that is three years after the completion of the Paragon.

The Revd Mr James died in 1793 owing Searles money and his son, a captain in the West Kent Militia, was not prepared to go ahead with the intended northern crescent. Taste in architecture may have been one reason. The pleasure which the Georgians derived from crescents may have faded, suggests W. Bonwitt, who has fully researched the subject for his book on the Paragon.

The residents saw their beautiful circus in jeopardy and asked Capt. James at least to increase the intervening space to ensure that the shared central garden would be rounder. But James refused and sold off the northern half in separate lots by auction in 1821. This became a terrace – called Gloucester Place until 1900 – and the destruction of Searles' original scheme ultimately came with bomb damage in the Second World War. Greenwich Council flats now occupy the terrace site and Gloucester Circus continues to be a misnomer for the one-sided crescent that never fulfilled its architect's ambition.

107. Nelson's body lying in state in the Painted Hall, Greenwich.

Greenwich in the Nineteenth Century

NELSON'S LYING-IN-STATE

Greenwich in the early nineteenth century was a small riverside town with a thinly-spread population of about 14,000 people mostly involved in waterfront occupations. No main road passed directly, as it does now, through the town from Woolwich to London. The town was somewhat isolated as it was bounded on the east by Greenwich Marsh and the approach from the west was impeded by Deptford Creek. The one unspoilt building of importance and a reminder of the town's historic past was the Royal Naval Hospital facing the Thames.

This peaceful isolation was suddenly broken when, after his death at Trafalgar in 1805, Nelson was brought home and his body carried ashore at Greenwich. His lying-in-state drew thousands to the town who had never been there before. They came with mixed feelings; the French were beaten but the joy of a great victory had been dulled by a sniper's bullet.

A State funeral was ordered by George III, and eleven weeks after Nelson's death the *Victory* sailed into the Thames Estuary commanded by Captain Hardy who had been on the quarterdeck with Nelson when he was hit. At Sheerness the coffin was transferred to a yacht which came up river to Greenwich with a salute of guns from forts at Tilbury and Gravesend. Vessels lined the route, their flags at half-mast. Sailors carried the body ashore, and Nelson was moved into the Painted Hall.

Preparations for the lying-in-state took ten days. The hall was hung with black draperies and lit by candles in silver sconces. As A.C. Pugin shows (107) the coffin was placed at the far end under a rich pall and in a semi-circle of candles.

The public's intense desire to pay personal tribute was demonstrated on Sunday, 5 January 1806. Before eight in the morning all roads to Greenwich were filled with vehicles bringing people to the Hospital. In scenes of confusion crowds of more than 10,000 struggled to get through the gates. These had to be closed, and were reopened with sailors carrying boarding pikes allowing fifty people at a time to come to the steps leading up to the Painted Hall. Passing up one side of the hall and down the other they saw Nelson's coffin, sombre, but with his

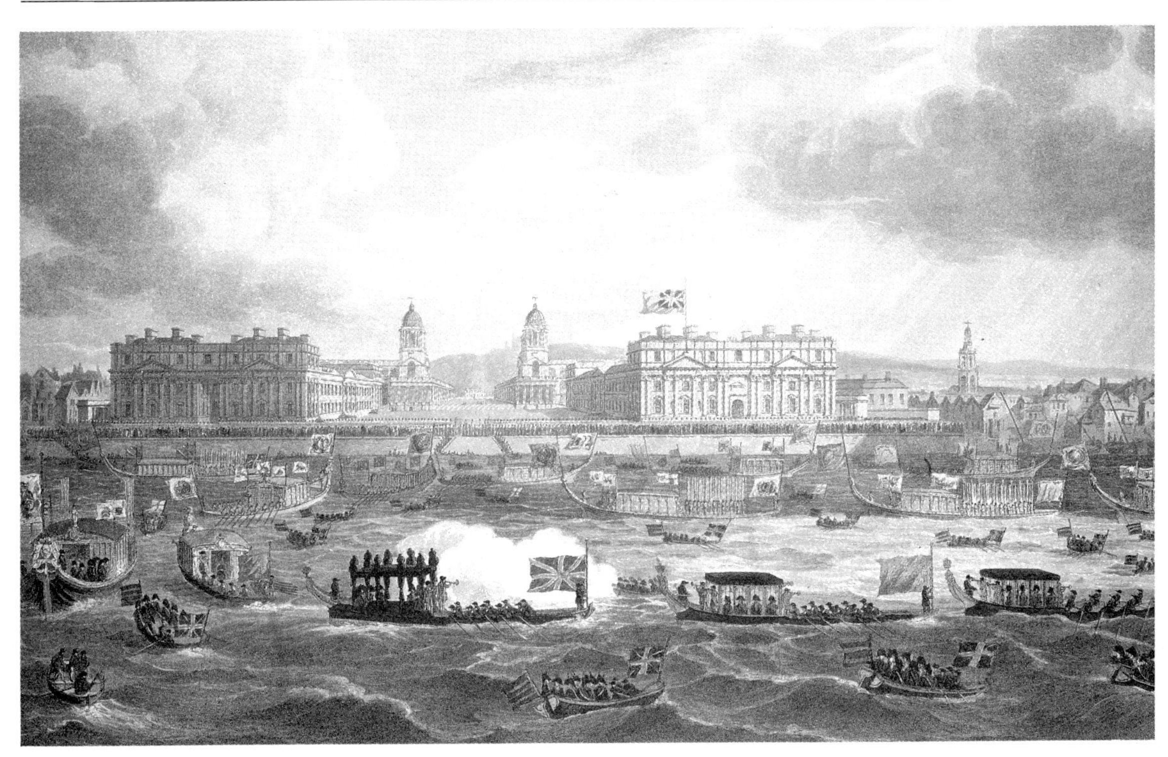

108. Nelson's funeral procession on the river at Greenwich. Aquatint by I. Hill after A.C. Pugin.

viscount's coronet brightly candlelit, state ornaments at the foot and his coat-of-arms at the head.

So large were the crowds that on the first day about 20,000 had to be turned away. On the third day the public was excluded for a short while so that sailors and mariners from *Victory* could visit their admiral's coffin in the company of his old commander, Admiral Lord Hood, by then Governor of Greenwich Hospital.

At midday on 8 January a gun fired from a boat on the river was the signal for Nelson's body to be taken in procession from the Painted Hall. Accompanied by 500 naval pensioners and a fife and drum band playing Handel's Dead March, the coffin was taken to the waterside and put aboard his barge from *Victory*. His personal crew of forty-six seamen were at the oars. Hood and another of Nelson's old commanders led the mourners. Ceremonial barges of the Lord Mayor and City companies moved into the floodtide in the wake of the funeral barge (108).

The river had been cleared of all shipping, but the black-draped flotilla made a difficult passage up stream buffeted by a south-westerly gale. Silent crowds lined the waterfront to see the journey that would end with the burial at St Paul's the following day. As Nelson started on his last voyage there came the dull thud of minute-guns fired from Greenwich.

109. Nineteenth-century painting of a mother and her son, a naval cadet, admiring a portrait of Nelson, entitled England's Pride and Glory, *by Thomas Davidson.*

110. Detail from a map of Greenwich, part of a parish survey made in 1834 by W.R. Morris.

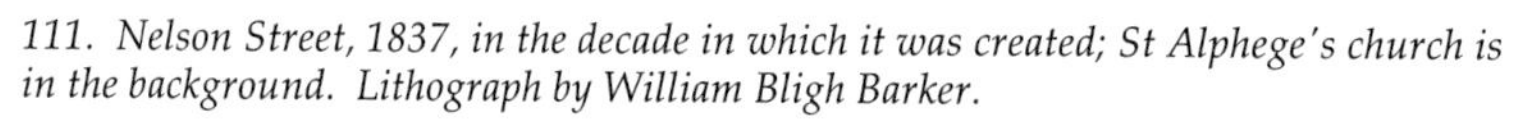

111. Nelson Street, 1837, in the decade in which it was created; St Alphege's church is in the background. Lithograph by William Bligh Barker.

CHANGES TO THE TOWN

Nelson and Trafalgar were names chosen for streets created in Greenwich in the 1830s as part of two very important changes. Until then the approach from London was circuitously long. The traveller coming by coach to Greenwich crossed the Ravensbourne near the *south* end of Deptford High Street, went down London Street as far as St Alphege's, the heart of Greenwich, then little more than a village.

If he was heading for the waterfront he carried on by foot up Church Street. To his left and right were small streets and alleys, the legacy of Tudor times. Only on Crooms Hill were a few big houses reminders of the fashionable seventeenth century.

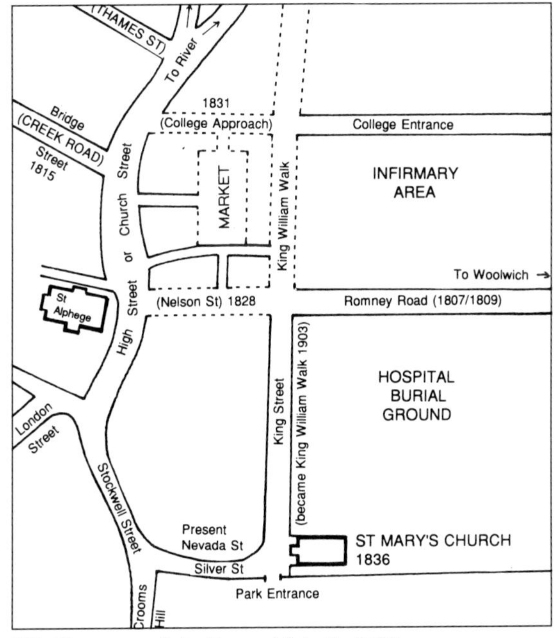

112. Changes made in Greenwich in the 1830s.

If the coach was carrying on to Woolwich, the route was devious and had to go round the main part of the town. Turning right at St Alphege's into Stockwell Street, the way led between the Spread Eagle Hotel and the Rose and Crown inn, along short Silver (now Nevada) Street, left into King Street (now King William Walk), and then turned right to make its way out of the town along present Romney Road.

Things changed radically when Nelson Street (now Nelson Road) was built in 1828 (111). This created a direct link from Romney Road through the town along Bridge Street (now Creek Road). By then Deptford Creek was no longer the impediment it had been for centuries. Deptford, known as West Greenwich, was now connected with the main town by an iron bridge, built in 1815. This replaced a wooden bridge of 1803 before which there had only been a ferry at the estuary end of the Ravensbourne.

The development that opened up Greenwich took place around 1830 and coincided with the time when the town became a parliamentary borough. The man responsible was the architect, Joseph Kay, who as Clerk of Works to Greenwich Hospital swept away congested areas of hospital property to create a town with a Regency look. A map of 1834 (110) and diagram (112) shows Kay's developments which so affected Greenwich. As well as creating the all-important Nelson Street, he built Clarence Street (now College Approach) in 1831 which, like King Street, was lined with attractively simple terraced houses. In his revolutionary changes to the town he also demolished clusters of small streets and courts to make room in 1829 for a new market for meat, fish and vegetables, a fine oblong building with an entrance in the style of a Greek colonnade.

The map which depicts the town three years before Queen Victoria's accession shows Greenwich in transition with fields dotted with houses and cottages and the faint outline of streets to come. Terraces can dimly be discerned on Royal Hill (named after Robert Royal, its principal developer), and south of Bridge Street. The time is approaching when Prior Street, Brand Street and Royal Hill will assume their modern appearance.

113. Visitors looking at pictures in the Painted Hall of Greenwich Hospital.

PENSIONERS SAY FAREWELL

By the middle of the nineteenth century the survivors of Trafalgar were mostly dead. Other veterans of the wars against France were becoming fewer and 400 beds at the Hospital were unoccupied by 1853. Other uses for the buildings had to be found.

More than 1,400 inmates accepted the offer of pensions when the Hospital closed in 1865. Many were pleased to do so because they found institutional life dull and preferred the freedom to go about and reside where they liked – perhaps with friends and relatives. Their departure occasioned much high-flown prose and nostalgic recollection. 'It was a pleasing sight on a fine day', one essayist recalled, 'to see the old pensioners standing about in groups or taking a solitary walk...intent, perchance, upon a book of adventures by sea that recalled the experiences of early life.' The 'noblest defenders of their country' were leaving the place where they had found their 'final port after the storms of a life of enterprise and danger'.

In October that year coaches rattled into the courtyard to collect the last remaining few – other than the very old and bedridden – to take some to other naval hospitals, a few to the villages of their youth.

After the exodus the main buildings stayed empty for four years. Then they found a new role. The Royal Naval College moved to Greenwich from Portsmouth. The King Charles block was converted into classrooms for naval students, Queen Mary's building into dormitories and mess rooms. Broadsides against 'dry-land seamanship' were fired by reactionaries, but sarcasm was soon forgotten. The Naval College became comfortably installed and, in a setting of some magnificence, officers began instructions 'in all branches of theoretical and scientific study'.

114. Old Pensioners leaving Greenwich Hospital; from the Illustrated London News, *21 October 1865.*

115. Children at the gate of the 'Asylum' for Naval Children.

'ASYLUM' FOR NAVAL CHILDREN

In its transition from a royal residence to the present museum, the Queen's House was occupied for 127 years by a school for naval children. Called an 'asylum' – that is institution – the building was used with such scant regard for Inigo Jones and the felicities of Palladian architecture that for nearly a century the north front was obscured by a fully rigged, aptly named, block ship (115).

The school for the sons and daughters of seamen was started in 1717, only twelve years after the Royal Hospital, and its original upkeep was met partly by money paid by visitors to the art gallery in the Painted Hall (113). In 1806 the school moved across Romney Road from the Hospital into the Queen's House which for several years previously had been in a poor way, neglected and mismanaged.

When the Crown disposed of the building, the school altered the inside to make classrooms, dormitories and quarters for the staff. Children who entered at twelve had to be orphans or motherless, their fathers disabled or serving abroad. In a mixed boarding school of 1,000 pupils, 300 were girls, a revolutionary concept at the time. Communicating door were kept constantly locked.

Aroused by the beat of a drum at 6 a.m., the boys were trained to be seamen. Great emphasis was placed on navigation, but they were taught so many trades that one Admiralty committee complained it was less a naval school than a large manufacturing establishment. At the turn of the century, however, as many as three-quarters of the boys went into the Navy. Girls in the early years had a less exalted training as servants.

With greatly enhanced twentieth-century prestige, the Royal Hospital School moved to Holbrook near Ipswich in Suffolk in 1933. With restored dignity, the Queen's House then became part of the National Maritime Museum.

GREENWICH FAIR

In the 1840s at the height of its popularity Greenwich Fair attracted large crowds at Easter and Whitsun. A fleet of fifty steamers from London came alongside the pier and during the day unloaded 150,000 people who swarmed through the streets in search of fun. It was an invasion not welcomed by residents who for more than a century had barred their doors against the 'rough merrymaking'.

Originally the fair had amounted to nothing more than high jinks in Greenwich Park and in booths set up in King William Walk. But the fair moved to wasteland along Bridge Street, extending as far as Deptford Creek, and in the new century became larger and increasingly ambitious.

John Richardson, the great itinerant showman who once had Edmund Kean among his performers, arrived annually and set up his booth. Gaudily clad actors paraded on a little stage in front of the entrance to entice audiences. He staged an overture, melodrama (with three murders and a ghost), a pantomime and a comic song - all in twenty minutes after which the booth was cleared for the next audience.

117. The steamboat pier at fair time, April 1843.

116. A mid-century Greenwich Fair

119. Scene from Greenwich Fair; detail from a drawing by A. Wray, c.1830.

Richardson's main competitor was Algar's Crown and Anchor Dancing Booth, possibly the earliest dance hall for the general public. As many as 2,000 people were able to dance in two areas of a large marquee while in a third area drinks were served. Wearing false noses, banging toy drums and with men and women swapping hats, dancers appeared to one observer to behave with 'complete abandon'.

Menageries were popular. George Wombwell presented lion and tiger taming acts and one year the 'Lion Queen' (daughter of a musician) was mauled to death in front of the audience. Sideshows held a constant appeal to the credulous. Curiosity could not resist fat ladies, bearded ladies, an ox with seven legs, a pig with two heads and - a great draw - a pig-faced woman (119).

Making itself heard above the general hubbub was a strange device known as a 'scratcher'. The scratcher (118) was a small hand roller described as a 'devastating and ingenious piece of mechanism'. The roller produced a noise 'resembling the laceration of a garment' and enjoyed a vogue in the 1840s. If a group of five or six girls made a joking attack on a hapless passer-by the noise was said to be enough to drive him into a frenzy.

Reports vary about 'the three-day fever' (as Dickens described Greenwich Fair). But Greenwich residents had no doubts. They complained that riotous crowds made it unsafe for their families to venture into the town. They mounted a campaign against 'the incentive to licentiousness among the middle and lower orders of the community'; they protested that the hours kept by booths were an offence 'against the best feelings of Christian morality'.

On Whit Sunday 1825 forty special constables ordered Richardson and a number of other stallholders to leave. Richardson moved on to Wandsworth, but when Algar's Dancing Booth refused to comply the constables decided not to carry out their threat to pull down the marquee.

Greenwich versus the Fair was a long drawn out war of attrition that went on until 1857. In that year 2,000 people put their objections to the Commissioner of Police. He issued an order not against the fair people but against the owners of the land who had let out spaces for booths along Bridge Street.

The land owners appealed to the local magistrate but he upheld the Commissioner's order. The *Greenwich Free Press* greeted this as the end of the 'market of Vice and Debauchery...The Battle is now won', the paper declared triumphantly.

118. Female attacked with a 'scratcher'.

120. Train on the line to Greenwich at Southwark Park Road.

Railway Mania

LONDON'S FIRST LINE

The expansion of Greenwich – a population increase of 20,000 in the fifty years up to 1851 – owed a great deal to the extraordinary engineering enterprise that took place in the 1830s. Straight as a Roman aqueduct, which it greatly resembled, supported on 878 arches, and running just under four miles from Southwark to Greenwich, London's first railway was the marvel of the age. A journey to the City taking an hour by coach was reduced to twelve minutes by the train which puffed over the fields and ditches to Spa Road, Bermondsey, and on to London Bridge.

The London and Greenwich Railway was conceived by a retired Royal Engineer, Colonel G.T. Landmann, who was born in Woolwich and spent much of his boyhood in Blackheath. Landmann served under Wellington in the Peninsular War and, in his early fifties, brought to his railway project a lifetime of adventure and enterprise which in his youth had included building a canal on the St Lawrence river.

122. Poster advertising the new railway.

Compared with cutting through Canadian mountains and valleys, negotiating suburban market gardens was child's play. But even so building a viaduct fifteen feet high to escape flooding in marshy ground and prevent the need for level crossings set a mammoth task. Nothing like it had ever been attempted before.

The railway required an estimated sixty million bricks, and before it was finished had cost the then astronomical sum of £1,000,000 – more than double the original estimate.

The first train ran in February 1836, and ten months later there were more celebrations when the extension to London Bridge was completed. The second opening was marked with the pomp and inevitable confusion of such events. At the midday start neither the guest of honour, the Lord Mayor of London, nor the locomotives to pull the carriages had arrived.

121. Train and private carriage on the line.

When he and the engines appeared there was a muddle about which special guests were to travel in which coaches. When this was sorted out bells rang out from parish churches along the way. In a banquet speech the Lord Mayor, making the kind of point dear to the City's heart, said the railway saved time and was important because 'time constitutes wealth'.

The spirit of the age – as well as the need to silence diehard critics of progress – required the railway to have an antiquarian flavour. So bridges were supported on Doric columns. At Deptford a stairway (demolished 1927) was inspired by a monument on the Acropolis. One carriage was shaped like a Roman galley. It was thought that the rich might like to bring their horses and carriages down from London for a turn in Greenwich Park and so a truck for carriages was attached to the train (121) and a gently sloping ramp for them to come down was built at Deptford.

Trees were planted to provide boulevards twenty-four feet wide on either side of the railway and pedestrians paid a small toll to stroll along them in 1839. The arches themselves were planned to contain little bijou villas but the scheme failed because they leaked and the noise of the trains was intolerable.

It was nearly another two years before the railway actually got to Greenwich. Before the destination was reached a special rail bridge had to be built across Deptford Creek.

Trains ran a fifteen-minute service and horse buses met the trains to take passengers on to Lewisham, Woolwich and Blackheath. Like the steamboats, the trains brought extra holidaymakers, and on Easter Monday 1841 as many as 7,000 arrived by rail in two hours; at the other end of the day return trains were needed until 2 a.m. to get people back to London.

Railway travel was not cheap. Large fares were required to get back the huge outlay. A single fare in a grand 'Imperial Carriage' was 1s. 0d. Standing in an open, seatless car cost 6d., and instead of a paper ticket a metal token was issued and collected at the end of each journey. Despite the expense of railway travel, by 1844 the Greenwich line was carrying more than two million passengers.

123. The Greenwich Railway which by 1841 had a spur line to New Cross and beyond.

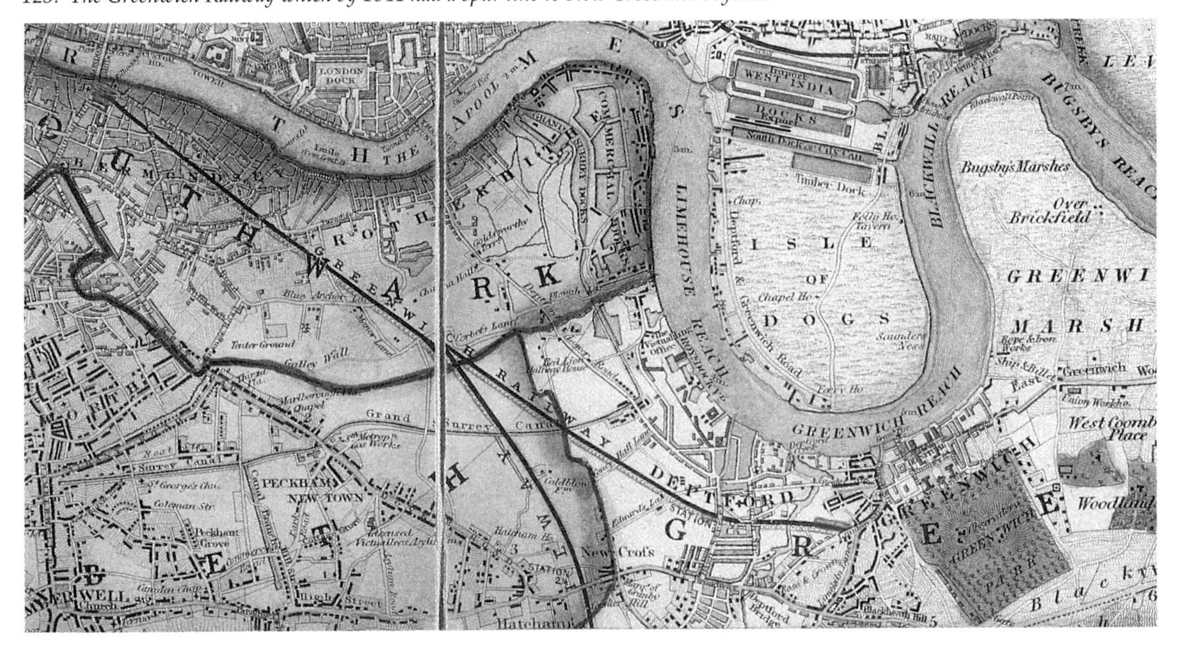

124. Small houses unsuccessfully planned under the arches.

125. The first permanent Greenwich station with roofed-over platform in 1858. Detail from a painting.

126. Proposed extension across the park. The train has been added to this 1835 print by a later hand.

EXTENSION OBSTRUCTED

Even while the London & Greenwich Railway was being built the promoters wanted to extend the line to Woolwich and Gravesend. But the idea of the railway crossing the park aroused intense opposition. It was bad enough, spluttered one local paper, to have 'this infernal Greenwich railway with all its thundering steam engines and omnibusters just ready to open, and ready to destroy, our rural town of Greenwich with red hot cinders and hot water...' But how intolerably worse, the paper went on, for the park to be invaded and peace shattered ≈ to connect with Gravesend of all places!

In an attempt to get local opinion on their side, the promoters produced a large print of an intended ornamental viaduct (126). Running parallel with the colonnade of the Queen's House, the viaduct was to be carried on dignified Tuscan columns. But this quasi-classical structure did not impress the Royal Naval Hospital, and an Admiralty representative is credited with obtaining an injunction requiring all copies of the print to be destroyed as illegal propaganda. A stream of objections followed. King William IV, his cousin Princess Sophia Matilda (as Honorary Ranger of the Park) and members of Parliament were petitioned and the Bill which authorized the extension was withdrawn.

But in the autumn of the same year, 1835, a new rail company continued the pressure. To forestall objections that the railway would disturb Greenwich Observatory, the company com-

127. Demolishing houses in King Street (now King William Walk)for the extension of the railway in 1875.

128. At Maze Hill station a head guard waves off a train before climbing into his 'birdcage' van with look-out window on the roof.

missioned a professor to carry out vibration tests. He reported that the Observatory would not be inconvenienced provided the Astronomer Royal signalled trains to halt for one minute every evening for delicate readings to be taken.

To get the naval authorities on their side, the promoters offered to place busts of celebrated admirals on the viaduct, leaving niches for future sea heroes, and erect in the centre 'a colossal statue of his present Majesty [William IV] in full naval uniform'.

It was too palpable a ploy, and the scheme was killed. Not until 1876 was the gap closed. This was achieved not by a viaduct of heroic scale but by a tactful tunnel that dived down under Greenwich High Road and burrowed below ground between the Queen's House and the Royal Naval College. Temporarily incommoded, buildings in King Street (127) were subsequently rebuilt.

Once the tunnel had been built under the park to Maze Hill the station there acquired an increased importance as it was now on a direct line for London. In 1890 Maze Hill Station carried the legend 'for East Greenwich', as if arrivals might be a bit bewildered and need to learn of the dual destination.

The line was certainly serving two very different communities. To the south were the large and prosperous houses on Maze Hill and Vanbrugh Hill and in Westcombe Park. It was to meet passengers who wanted to be carried up the hill that four wheel 'growlers' waited outside the station on Westcombe Park in 1885 and a similar service was provided by a hansom at Greenwich Station in the same year (130).

There are not likely to be many cab fares to the small workmen's houses that lie across Trafalgar and Woolwich roads to the north. This is a congested 'New Town' that sprang up during the nineteenth century with small houses for people working in industries that developed on East Greenwich Marsh. Maze Hill Station has a web of sidings, but no passenger line runs up the marshy peninsula to Blackwall Point. There are only a few freight lines serving small factories, engineering and gas works and wharves on Bugsby's Reach.

Despite Blackwall Tunnel linking East Greenwich with the Essex side of the river in 1897, the only public transport on the Marsh until 1906 was a horse bus running from Deptford and Greenwich through the tunnel to Poplar.

129. An 'elegant omni' - a Shillibeer omnibus of the kind serving Greenwich.

130. Waiting for the trains in 1885. A hansom at Greenwich and 'growlers' serving Westcombe Park.

SHILLIBEER FIGHTS THE RAILWAYS

Horse-drawn vehicles fought tenaciously against the trains and in 1834 - a year before the opening of the railway - George Shillibeer, an omnibus pioneer born in Tottenham Court Road, working as a coach builder in Paris decided to bring buses to London. His first service ran from Paddington to Bank, but faced with serious competition in north London, he began a service between Greenwich and London. Operating from headquarters in the Old Kent Road, he had sixteen vehicles and 120 horses. His buses seated fifteen people. In his battle for passengers Shillibeer asked a popular songwriter to help and one verse ran:

> 'That the beauties of Greenwich and Deptford may ride
> In his elegant omni is the height of his pride
> So the plan for a railroad must soon disappear
> While the public approve of the new Shillibeer.'

But the railway did not disappear and Shillibeer also had to fight the river steamers which started a cut rate fare to Greenwich and on to Woolwich. When he failed to pay government mileage duty all his property was seized. He fled to France, returned to fight his case but was imprisoned in the Fleet. Subsequently Shillibeer managed to conduct tolerably successful road services. The pioneer of the service to Greenwich died in 1866 and was buried in Chigwell where he is remembered by a tablet in the church which - with a little exaggeration - calls him the 'inventor of the London Omnibus'.

GHOST LINE

Abandoned railway lines and vanished stations leave ghostly tracks through London's suburbs. One of the strangest is a line which opened in 1888 and existed in a tentative, unconvincing way for only about seventy years. The line - a curved spur two-and-a- quarter miles long - ran from Brockley Lane to a terminus at Greenwich Park Station. The station was across the road from St Alphege's Church.

An outcome of railway mania in mid-Victorian times, the line has now so disappeared that it can only be traced by diligent exploration. The cuttings through which the track ran were filled in to street level about thirty years ago. But small sections of this ghost line still haunt residents who would like to acquire the overgrown wasteland at the end of their gardens.

The line into Greenwich Park Station was authorized in 1863 when its only plausible purpose was to carry people across south-east London to the Crystal Palace. True, trains could branch off beyond Lewisham Road Station through to London but this was an unnecessarily circuitous route. It may have been perceived that the number of people who would want to travel from Greenwich to the Crystal Palace would be limited because lack of finance delayed the opening until 1888.

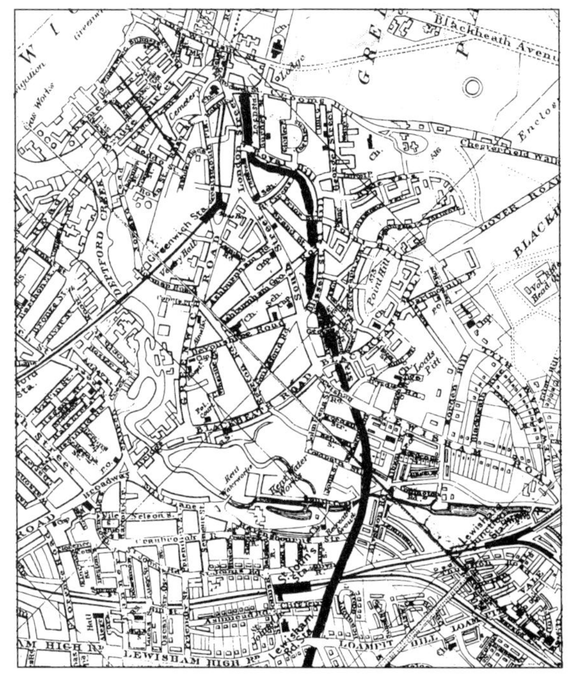

132. The ghost line.

131. Blackheath Hill Station at the end of its life.

133. A tram en route between Greenwich and Westminster, 1885.

From Greenwich Park Station the line went through two cuttings and a short tunnel which skirted Gloucester Circus, crossed Royal Hill and cut a swathe through back gardens before passing into a tunnel under Blackheath Hill, where there was a station (131), now demolished.

In 1917 the line was closed as an economy measure and, although reopened, it faced a doomed future. A bomb fell on the line during the Second World War (p. 133). Subsequently the terminus became a billiard club and by the 1960s the station had become a timber yard. Today the Ibis Hotel stands on the site.

In retrospect this ghost line appears an infinitely less practical means of transport than the horse tram seen resolutely setting out for town from Trafalgar Road in 1885 (133), the year the line was being built. With forty seats and a 'knife-board' back- to-back on top, it charged 4d. for the six-and-a-quarter-mile journey to Westminster. Horse trams were superseded by electric trams in the century to come. A means of travel they seem in retrospect almost as improbable as the Ornithopter seen over Greenwich Park. This fantasy by an artist in 1843 (see title-page) envisages a journey home at the end of the day less crowded than the railway.

Mr Spurgeon's People

On Boxing Night, 1885, the Revd Charles Spurgeon, Baptist minister of Greenwich South Street, gave a lantern lecture entitled 'Street Characters and Cries'. He had been preparing his talk since the previous August bank holiday when he and a photographer had gone out to take pictures.

Charles Spurgeon was a son of the famous Baptist preacher, Charles Haddon Spurgeon, who drew thousands to his Metropolitan Tabernacle, Elephant and Castle. He came to Greenwich in 1879 and his unique collection of photographs provides a social study to be set alongside Mayhew and Booth. But although an active evangelist, he probably did not intend anything so significant. He seems less of a social critic than a dispassionate observer. Although he shows a few ragged children, the tone is amiable.

Perhaps the most famous of Spurgeon's photographs was of a barefoot young match seller (135). He is selling slow-burning 'Alpine Vesuvian' matches (1d a box of 20) and is probably one in the teams of boys, mostly ill-treated and badly housed, which were organised by stern overseers. To Victorian humanists the picture had a special appeal; the boy's stance with one foot out of the gutter was interpreted as meaning that with perseverance and industry he could rise in the world.

Most of some fifty studies depict kerbside traders selling anything from sherbert drinks to old clothes. Watched by a socially very different boy, the man below (90) brings rabbits caught locally to Greenwich front doors and wears a bit of sacking to keep blood off his coat. A blind fiddler with his dog outside Crowder's Music Hall (p. 101) is another of Spurgeon's social masterpieces.

134. Rabbits for sale. Greenwich street vendor in 1885.

135. A small boy selling matches in the streets with, symbolically, one foot on the pavement and the other in the gutter.

136. Blackheath Station designed with classical simplicity, probably by George Smith, the Blackheath architect.

Blackheath Expands

The railway reached Blackheath in 1849, eleven years after Greenwich. The line from London made its way through a natural valley and then went on to Woolwich and Gravesend. As if sensitive to the

137. Growlers in Tranquil Vale by the shelter for cabmen built by grateful residents.

138. Tilling horse buses from Blackheath at the Old and New Tiger's Head, Lee.

scenery, a tunnel took trains under Morden College and deep cuttings so little disturbed the landscape that only five houses had to be pulled down on the extension towards Charlton.

As far as the village was concerned Blackheath was only made conscious of trains by a low rumble and engine smoke rising above the bridge at the bottom of Tranquil Vale. The tracks were masked by a simple and elegant station.

The more general effect, however, on what until then had been scarcely more than a sleepy village was considerable. No longer restricted to those with private carriages or prepared to face a long horse-bus journey to London, Blackheath became an ideal place to live.

With the centre of London only twenty minutes away once Charing Cross opened in 1864, Blackheath's popularity further increased and houses began to spread rapidly over the Cator Estate and south of Belmont Hill.

At first horse bus operators viewed trains with alarm, but while there was a decline in long-haul services, omnibuses and cabs continued to run from the station. For the last part of the journey home growlers were lined up in Tranquil Vale (137) and friends from the City paused for a word before hiring them (139).

The Thomas Tilling buses at the south end of Lee Road (138) were part of interlinking town and station services, and these served the Blackheath-Eltham route from 1867 to 1907. As London's largest transport company, Tilling needed extensive stabling and opened depots in Old Road, Lee, in Blackheath off Pond Road, and in Grotes Place. In the new century Tilling along with other independent companies became motorized and the last horse bus in Blackheath ran in 1912.

139. 'Consuls held up well today...' An affable chat before the journey home.

140. Carriage trade in Blackheath at the turn of the century.

141. Half-a-mile away gypsies claiming roving rights made their encampment off Belmont Hill. Their caravans were probably in Heath Lane by the grounds of a rich family mansion, The Cedars

142. Postcard to her aunt from a girl at the High School.

GROVES OF ACADEME

Blackheath High School for girls, with a reputation for teaching classics, had reason to be envious of one particular achievement of a boys' school nearby. In 1883 Blackheath Proprietary School staged a comedy by Aristophanes in the original Greek. The performance took place not in the amphitheatre at Epidaurus but at the Roller Skating Rink in Blackheath Grove.

The High School had been going only three years at this date and appears to have weathered the academic set-back. The girls have survived, while the Proprietary School closed its doors in 1907. Now built over by Selwyn Court, the 'Prop' deserves a more fitting memorial than a group of 1930s' shops and flats named after the Revd Edward John Selwyn, its early headmaster. A public school without boarders which opened in 1831, its reputation was once formidable. Selwyn and his successors turned out boys who became bishops, generals (one conceived the tank in the First World War), members of Parliament, countless civil servants and gowned academics. Less loudly perhaps, the school acclaimed Donald McGill of the comic seaside postcards on its roll of honour.

In a hearty world where the shout of 'School! School!' is roared on Saturday afternoon touchlines, the Proprietary School continues to be remembered even though its last old boy has long ceased to limp his way to Rectory Field to cheer Blackheath Rugby Club which the school more or less founded.

Why such a notable school declined and lost numbers is not clear. People say the name 'Proprietary' was confusing (it merely meant that many parents had shares); a more likely reason is that it was a day school in an area where boys were generally sent to boarding schools.

On the other hand Blackheath High School continues to thrive as it always has done on a traditional curriculum which includes Latin and Greek. Success came from the start because of the school's aims. When the High School opened in 1880 in an undistinguished little side street off Montpelier Row, preparing girls for universities and the professions was unusual. But it was an idea that matched the aspirations of an area with art schools, a conservatoire and a concert hall. Here was the kind of academy which enlightened Blackheath parents wanted for their daughters. Fees were according to means regardless of social position. Naturally the 'Bastable girls' (in E.N. Nesbit's famous novels) attended. The school has never pretended to be anything but conservative, but is happy to recall that it backed women's suffrage (non-militantly) in its day. From under the proud classical portico in Wemyss Road, ninety per cent of the girls go out each year to universities or other places of higher education.

143. Morden Grange, as originally built, and below (144) decapitated and converted into a bungalow..

BARONIAL BUNGALOW

On the eastern fringes of the Heath, Kidbrooke remained rural longer than the rest of Blackheath. Named after two brooks, tributaries of the Kid rising on Shooters Hill, Kidbrooke, once with an ancient manor house, consisted of agricultural land. Most survived until the 1850s, some as late as 1925. About 500 acres were leased to three farmers by the earls of St German, whose family came into the property in the eighteenth century.

Though the name looms large with St German's Place overlooking the Heath, they were absentee landlords with their family seat in Cornwall. Despite increasing land values near London, the estate held out against selling. The first land they let go for building was along Shooters Hill Road; then plots were sold for the creation of Kidbrooke Park Road.

As more people came to live in this area of Blackheath, homes were built on such idyllically named pastures as Swinging Gate Field, Merry Field and Four Acre Field. And, as if to raise a memorial to a past that was slipping away, Morden Grange appeared in 1888.

Built in large grounds at the end of a 100-yard drive, the Grange testified to the Victorian veneration of baronial life. Mullioned windows, massive front door, grand staircase and a great hallway with obligatory stag's head all hinted heavily at a Tudor origin. But, in fact, this seemingly ancestral pile was

the creation of a manager of the London Stock Exchange. Richard Winch commissioned an architect not averse to pastiche, John Belcher, to design a mansion which a friend who went to tea with the daughter of the house declared to be 'all very substantial and comfortable'.

Winch enjoyed his fantasy home for twenty-eight years. Described as 'generous and sympathetic' (in his obituary), he made up in local beneficence what he lacked in lineage. He was also a music lover, amateur golfer and active Conservative. He had at least five children to fill the Grange's twenty-two rooms. But when he died in 1918 the aftermath of his dream home was cruel. The mansion was sold three years later and divided in half, not vertically, but with the upper storey and crenellated parapets sliced off. The Grange became a bungalow, its drive and grounds obliterated. And so it remains with ivy clinging on defiantly as a reminder of the past.

POLITICS ON THE HEATH

The clash of politics is not a sound with which Blackheath is particularly familiar. Things have been fairly quiet since Wat Tyler's day. A report has it that a red flag was hung from a window in Tory Kidbrooke during an election in the 1930s, but an elderly resident declares that this dangerous symbol was quickly removed. As might be expected, Greenwich has rather more fire in its veins. With a big working class electorate and an infusion of radical young professionals, there is increased political activity.

Spread over the years of the last century Chartists, temperance reformers and suffragettes were all heard on the Heath but it took bonfires and fireworks to draw big crowds. These were reserved for occasions like Queen Victoria's Diamond Jubilee (150) and the Relief of Mafeking. The tradition of firework displays goes back to the Fall of Sebastapol during the Crimean War. This took place a year after the event and Blackheath was criticised by the *Illustrated London News* for being dilatory. The probable reason is that it took some financing because 'Nobility, Gentry and the Public in general' were invited to attend a special meeting (146) and asked to subscribe to the 'Grand Demonstration'. But the writer of the attack finally praised the 'brilliant display of fireworks' and a bonfire which he said produced 'a bright and ruddy show', illuminating the faces of some 30,000 spectators.

FALL OF SEBASTOPOL.

TO THE

Nobility, Gentry, and Public in general.

GRAND

DEMONSTRATION

At a Meeting of the Committee, held at Mr. POOLE'S, Princess of Wales, Blackheath, it was resolved that a

PUBLIC MEETING

SHOULD TAKE PLACE AT THE

LECTURE HALL,

BLACKHEATH,

On Monday Evening, September 24th, 1855,

AT SEVEN O'CLOCK,

When all Parties favourable to carrying out the same are invited to attend.

The Public are respectfully requested not to subscribe to any one but the Committee, who will give each person a printed Receipt; and

146. *Poster for a meeting to raise a public subscription to mark the Fall of Sebastopol*

145. *Fireworks on the Heath to celebrate the Fall of Sebastopol. From the* Illustrated London News, *October 1855.*

Around the same time far less attractive demonstrations were made against Roman Catholics. Protestors murmured angrily when the Church of Our Lady Star of the Sea appeared on Crooms Hill in 1851, and two years later an assault on 'Papism' took a more violent form when an 18 ft effigy of the Pope was given a ritual burning on the Heath. According to one wild story a cardinal dining in St German's Place made an escape from rioters only by climbing over a garden wall.

In 1842 a crowd of 50,000 went to hear Father Theobald Mathew, a noted temperance reformer, and Lord Palmerston was among them. Some 500 signed the pledge in the face of barracking by hooligans and Royal Marines who, emerging from beer tents that had been set up with the intention of creating trouble, shouted down the speaker.

The Chartists appeared twice on the Heath, once with Feargus O'Connor as a fervent speaker, and four years later when a smaller rally cheered a demand for universal suffrage and the speaker whipped up the crowd with the exhortation: 'We shall not be terrified with bullets and bayonets' and by an impassioned reference to his listeners as 'oppressed and starving men' threatened by 'tyrants in the ascendant'. 'Nothing short of universal suffrage will satisfy

148. Sandwich-board men on the Heath.

147. Gladstone speaking on the Heath at the 1868 election.

the nation,' he told them to resounding cheers.

Of the few parliamentary political meetings on the Heath the most interesting was W.E. Gladstone's in 1868. A rare early photograph shows him being introduced to his electors at the hustings (147). It was an emergency occasion. For all his eminence as Liberal leader in the House, Mr Gladstone had been defeated in south-west Lancashire. Greenwich simultaneously came to the rescue and adopted him. As soon as his victorious return was known a local printer ran off a poster (151) on which Gladstone thanked his new constituents for their 'generous, unasked and I believe unparalleled kindness'. Ten days later Greenwich had the satisfaction of hearing that their MP had been summoned to Windsor. He was the new prime minister.

The Heath heard Gladstone again. He chose Blackheath to deliver a non-stop two-hour speech in 1871 defending his government's policies. An artist was there to depict the large corps of reporters presumably working in relays to take down his speech. He returned five years later in 1876 to speak in protest against Turkish atrocities in Bulgaria.

149. Mr Gladstone speaking at Blackheath in 1871.

150. A bonfire on Blackheath to celebrate Queen Victoria's Jubilee, 1897.

151. Mr Gladstone's thanks to the voters of Greenwich after the 1868 election.

TO THE ELECTORS

OF THE

BOROUGH OF GREENWICH.

LIVERPOOL, Nov. 25, 1868.

GENTLEMEN,

It has up to this day been my duty to with-hold any expression of my gratitude for your generous, unasked, and, I believe unparalleled kindness, which at this important juncture has given me a most honourable seat in Parliament.

Yesterday about One o'clock I became aware that I should probably be able to accept the trust you have tendered to me: and I now lose no time in accepting it with my cordial and respectful thanks.

It was not Gentlemen any mere professions or promises of mine, which won from you this signal favour; and it is not by professions or promises, but by my conduct in Parliament, that I humbly hope to show it has not been unworthily bestowed.

I have the honour to remain,

GENTLEMEN,

Your most obliged and faithful Servant,

W. E. GLADSTONE.

152. The Green Man at the top of Blackheath Hill as it looked until about 1868.

Art, Music and Entertainment

For nearly 300 years the Green Man tavern and hotel stood at the top of Blackheath Hill. Pleasantly inviting, with bow windows and pillared entrance, this was the legendary hostelry as most people would like to imagine it (152). Unfortunately no one is still alive who can remember it like this; it was replaced in 1870 by a ponderous Victorian building which stood for a century and now a modern block of flats, Alison Close, stands on the site.

But the history of the Green Man cannot easily be effaced. Before Blackeath was large enough to need assembly rooms of its own, the hotel served as a centre for just about everything. John Evelyn saw it adjoining a bowling green when it opened around 1683. Golfers, archers and political parties held banquets there. The Assembly Rooms were used for balls, concerts, lectures and military drilling. Madame Tussaud staged her travelling waxwork show there in 1833 and, more prosaically, it was used by Blackheath as a postal collection point.

Not surprisingly the Green Man lured away the clientele of a rival establishment, the Chocolate House, on the other side of the main Shooters Hill Road, which closed down after being fashionable for most of the eighteenth century. Perhaps customers preferred something stronger than chocolate.

The Green Man also echoed to rowdy choruses and the chairman's gavel for it was licensed for music hall performances from 1850 until 1902. These would have been the 'free-and-easy' shows which many public houses put on several nights a week.

For music hall on a more ambitious scale, and with big names on the bill, people went down to Greenwich. In 1855 two variety halls opened. One was the oddly named Good Duke Humphrey Coffee Tavern which seated about 700 at 15 Park Row; the other, roughly the same size, was the Rose and Crown at the bottom of Crooms Hill. Eleven years later Charles Morton, famous for his management of the Canterbury and Oxford music halls, opened 'Morton's', also a 700-seater, in London Road (site of the 1930s' Town Hall) and this existed until 1911.

The great survivor and most celebrated of the three was the Rose and Crown. Under eight different names that included Greenwich Palace of Varieties, Parthenon and Greenwich Hippodrome, it has survived down the years to be transformed into the Greenwich Theatre of today.

Changes followed very much in the nineteenth-century music hall tradition. First there was a large room where in the 1850s shows took place in the same building as the public house but not under its direct auspices. Then John Green, licensee of the Rose and Crown, applied for a music licence and the variety theatre came into being.

Charles Crowder was the next important name, billed large on the wall in Silver Street (153) where he largely rebuilt the theatre in 1871. In the great period to come Marie Lloyd, Vesta Tilley and Harry Champion all appeared. When he was on the bill at Greenwich, Dan Leno sometimes lodged at the Spread Eagle inn across the street. The great music hall of the 1880s became a 'picture palace' in the 1920s,

153. Blind fiddler outside Crowder's music hall: one of Spurgeon's photographs.

closed in 1949 and for thirteen years remained a municipal warehouse threatened with demolition. Derelict with flaking gilt work and a cherub looking down from the proscenium on a clutter of furniture, the theatre cried out to be saved.

Rescue was largely due to the superhuman efforts of the actor Ewan Hooper who undertook the theatre's renaissance in 1962. The start of his plan coincided with the departure from Stratford East of Joan Littlewood, who left in despair when her Theatre Workshop company foundered. It was not a good auspice, and suggested that, however splendid the conception, the chances of a repertory company on the edge of London were fragile. But Hooper still went ahead. Greenwich Borough Council, the GLC and the Arts Council all helped but to collect the £88,000 needed people in the whole area, on housing estates as well as owners of prosperous homes, were canvassed. Hooper's vision was a classless 'community theatre' not relying on West End patrons. The most successful fund-raising came from 'olde tyme' music hall performances staged at the Green Man.

154. The Greenwich Theatre before its modern renovation.

Seven years later Hooper took over the directorship and, even if his egalitarian hopes were not fulfilled, during his regime Greenwich Theatre (designed with great flair by a local architect, Brian Meeking) became an outstanding London fringe playhouse and this continued when a new company was formed in 1973 by Robin Phillips.

The excitement of the music hall's heyday in the 1870s magically returned almost exactly a century later with a theatre that staged new plays by Alan Ayckbourn, John Mortimer and Peter Nichols. Glenda Jackson, Susan Hampshire and (emerging from retirement) Elisabeth Bergner were among stars eager to appear at Greenwich. With characteristic ingenuity, Jonathan Miller unified *Ghosts, The Seagull* and *Hamlet* under the title of *Family Romances*.

155. *John Townsend, actor and M.P.*

THE ACTING MEMBER

An evening in Greenwich which arouses some speculation took place at the Royal Hill Lecture Hall in 1866. Posters announced Mr John Townsend and his wife in a 'Dramatic Entertainment' together with their fourteen year-old son Master H. Townsend ('unanimously pronounced the most accomplished Juvenile Swordsman of the day').

All 900 seats were taken not because *Richard III* was a draw but out of curiosity to see Townsend who had formerly been their Member of Parliament. This very unusual character, the son of a prosperous Deptford auctioneer, had gone on the stage as a boy, and leased the Theatre Royal, Richmond, after Edmund Kean's regime before touring with his own stock company. When his father died Townsend gave up the theatre and at the age of thirty-three returned to carry on the family business.

At this point his lifestyle changed radically. He became a Poor Law guardian. He fought to raise dockers' pay. Even more unexpectedly he was elected MP for Greenwich. But then his affairs went badly wrong. An actor's life had not prepared him for the enmity of fierce business competition. He was forced into bankruptcy and had to give up his parliamentary seat.

But even before he applied for 'the Chiltern Hundreds' and while still a MP, Townsend decided to return to his old love. In the late 1850s he played Shylock at Marylebone Theatre to 'deafening applause' (*Morning Star*). His Richard III received 'long and prolonged cheers' at Rochester, and in 1858 at Astley's Royal Amphitheatre he gave Richard an added equestrian flavour by appearing with dramatic aplomb on the horse he was to lose at the Battle of Bosworth. He is said to have been the last theatre actor to play Richard III on horseback.

Illness at forty decided Townsend to emigrate. The rousing Whit Monday 'benefit' performance on Royal Hill (which raised £200) was his farewell to his former constituents before he and his family left for Canada. There he started a fresh stage career which lasted until his retirement in 1877. A fragile poster at Greenwich local history library remains the acting member's tattered memorial.

CULTURE ON THE HEATH

Whatever gaudy nights were celebrated at the Green Man and behind gas footlights down in Greenwich, in Blackheath a sober, more cultural note was struck. The nearest Blackheath came to music hall was Albert Chevalier singing *My Old Dutch*, sanctified because the coster comedian had given a Royal Command performance at Windsor. The nearest to popular musical evenings were unremitting productions of Gilbert and Sullivan by the Amateur Operatic Society.

Greenwich, in fact, had a head start on Blackheath in the pursuit of culture with the foundation of the Philharmonic Society in 1834 and soon afterwards started the Society for the Acquisition and Diffusion of Useful Knowledge with reading rooms and a centre for further education. A great coup was to secure Charles Dickens to give one of his dramatic readings at the Greenwich Literary Institute on Royal Hill.

Blackheath was not far behind. As more people came to live in big houses around the village there was an increasing call for the kind of pastimes enjoyed by the prosperous middle classes. In 1845 this led to the village building its own Literary Institution with a lecture hall, lending library and reading room. This building with tall windows overlooked the railway station. It opened daily at 8 a.m. to give travellers a chance to look at *The Times* before catching their train to London.

The lecture hall was large enough for song and instrumental recitals, talks (learned enough to embrace the plays of Schiller), magic lantern shows and performances by the Blackheath Sacred Harmonic Society. The village could feel a comfortable satisfaction that it now had a place for assemblies that would have been unthinkable at the Green Man.

Taking its name from Princess Alexandra of Denmark (whose engagement to the future Edward VII had just been announced) the Alexandra Assembly Rooms were opened in 1863 in Cresswell Park (site of the present Lloyd's Bank). There was a reading room (in Grecian style) and concerts were held at night. By day courses in Italian, the harp, philosophy and

156. Blackheath Concert Hall on the right of the Conservatoire of Music.

callisthenics were available 'for the daughters of Gentlemen only'.

The Alexandra Hall had a short life but was a prelude to a series of ambitious activities enjoyed by Blackheath in the twilight of the Victorian age. Forget the healthy advent of Harding's Tepid and Swimming Baths (Cresswell Park, 1863); ignore the metallic hum of the Roller Skating Rink (Blackheath Grove, 1876); fuller concentration is deserved by the Blackheath Academy of Art (1877), the Conservatoire of Music (1881) and the Blackheath Art Club (1883).

The inauguration of all these enlightened institutions reached a musical crescendo in 1895 with the opening of the Blackheath Concert Hall. Able to seat 1,200, and with a crowning position on the hill at the corner of Lee Road and Blackheath Park, this had a claim to being London's only purpose-built concert hall. The fine new building brought famous musicians to Blackheath. Among them were the composer Percy Grainger, the pianist Mark Hambourg and the violinist Fritz Kreisler. Samuel Coleridge-Taylor came to a performance of his *Hiawatha*; there was awed admiration for an eleven year-old prodigy, the pianist Solomon; it was to be expected that Dame Clara Butt would not be let off the stage until she had given full voice to *Land of Hope and Glory*.

In Edwardian times the Concert Hall was not reserved exclusively for music. Edward Shackleton lectured on the Antarctic; Bernard Shaw came to plead the cause of the National Theatre; Tango Teas were a lively introduction to the Jazz Age. In thirty-six years after 1893 an incorrigibly enthusiastic Blackheath Amateur Dramatic Society put on eighty-eight productions and one of its young members was H.M. Tennant, the future West End impresario.

One event which could well have been a fond farewell to such aristocratic presumptions as the village possessed was a Coronation Ball when George V became king. A newspaper report that the lowly crowded outside the Concert Hall to watch Blackheath's 'leading 300 families' arrive in diamonds and carriages, leads to speculation about who were these élite.

157. The Literary Institution, Blackheath.

158. Pause in play: a Medal Day player in 1874 waits for a warning flag to be lowered as a coach passes.

Fun and Games on Blackheath

INVASION BY GOFFERS

King James I came from Scotland and Scotland is the country where golf – or goff as it was called – was played as early as the fifteenth century. It has therefore been assumed that James enjoyed the game.

James intermittently occupied Greenwich Palace, and it would only have been natural for the King and his courtiers to go up on the Heath and swing a club. On this premise is based an assumption that Blackheath is the oldest golf club in England.

Into the controversy has crept the year 1609 as the date when 'a Society of Golfers' was formed (no written proof) with, it is said, royal approval (absolutely no proof). But they were enough for Blackheath Golf Club boldly to call itself 'Royal', an addition made in 1857 (without benefit of a charter) in the heady aftermath of beating the Royal and Ancient at St Andrews by seven holes. In 1901 the Crown bestowed the formal accolade.

Much of this has to be tentative because the early records of the club were destroyed at the end of the eighteenth century and no one appears to have had the sense to make a note of what they said.

The actual foundation of the club was probably in the 1740s and the undisputed written story began in 1787 when the club met at a sporting rendezvous, the Chocolate House, in the Grove at the Blackheath Hill end of Shooters Hill Road. Most of the members had

159. A golfer plays to a gallery in 1893.

160. The putter: players with glengarries testify to the tradition of Scottish membership in the Blackheath Golf Club.

Scottish names and a contemporary newspaper account is colourful:

> 'On Saturday a fine game of Goff was played upon Blackheath, by upwards of 30 gentlemen of the London Scots Society, dressed in uniforms, in scarlet jackets and white waistcoats. The fineness of the day and the picturesque appearance of the players, with their attendants in blue, continually moving in small parties over the heath, rendered it a sight highly pleasing...'

161. William Innes, captain of the Society of Goffers, Blackheath, in 1792. Morden College is in the background.

The game was played every Saturday from April to November with dinner afterwards at the Chocolate House and this continued until 1792 when the club moved across the main Shooters Hill Road to the Green Man public house.

The gravel pits overgrown with gorse, sunken roads and ponds made natural hazards for the course. Five holes were increased to seven in 1844. Caddies were recruited from Greenwich pensioners until the Naval Hospital was closed in 1865.

Before the end of the century the game was being played by women who established the Royal Blackheath Ladies Golf Club with their own clubhouse at No. 3 Montpelier Row. They wore red hat ribbons, and a red coat for danger was adopted by the men players. 'Golfers must wait for people and conveyances to pass out of their way before playing', was a rule, and a late nineteenth-century engraving (158) shows the delay when a coach is driving across the fairway.

When the Heath was requisitioned for a military depot in 1914 all play stopped and the club moved to Eltham. The Blackheath visitors merged with the Eltham Golf Club in 1923 and the fine seventeenth-century Eltham Lodge designed by Hugh May became the mutual clubhouse.

Although golf could not continue on the Heath some members took over Heath Hill House, changed its name to Golf House and used it as a club until the 1950s. Members clung to an arcane right to practice shots before 8.00 a.m., a right which the chairman of the amenity group, the Blackheath Society, successfully tested in recent years.

162. Pedestrianism. Aquatint by Rowlandson.

OTHER SPORTS

A record exists of a wrestling match 'holden upon Blake Hethe besyde London' in 1373 when one of the wrestlers was killed, and ever since that fatal occasion a great variety of sports have taken place on the Heath. One of the most curious was Pedestrianism in which people set themselves the target of walking a fixed distance in a limited time. Rowlandson shows us this money-raising activity in about 1795 with the Green Man public house in the background (162).

The most celebrated walker was George Wilson, 'the Blackheath Pedestrian', who in 1815 announced his intention of walking 1,000 miles in 1,000 hours. Fearing that crowds of spectators might be a threat, the authorities stopped the walk and Wilson was taken before the magistrates on the charge of walking for money on a Sunday.

Accounts exist of running (between milestones for bets); horse trotting (with wagers on whether a horse could walk, trot and gallop ten miles in an hour); even races involving people picking up stones were occasional pastimes. Archery was popular in the 1780s with an 'elegant and beauteous assembly of Lady Archers'. Tom Cribb from Woolwich was only one of many prizefighters who fought on Blackheath. A rough Highland game called Shinty (a kind of wild hockey), was played in the 1840s and later more traditional hockey was introduced.

Hockey, football and lacrosse were all seen on the Heath and five schools regularly used the open space as free playing fields.

Between 1872 and 1912 riding schools used a 'Rotten Row' by Pond Road. Blackheath Harriers, founded in 1857, made the Green Man their base. Rifle clubs have shot in the gravel pits with targets below parapet level. In 1943 baseball was played by United States servicemen. It is hard to name a sport not enjoyed at some time on south-east London's giant recreation ground.

163. Wilson walking.

164. Blackheath Rugby Football Club, 1862.

WAS THIS THE FIRST RUGGER SIDE?

The faded picture above hangs proudly in the Rectory Field headquarters of Blackheath Football Club. It is 'one of the most famous photographs in football history', according to Neil Rhind who has meticulously researched the subject. But he queries its authenticity. Whoever mounted and captioned the picture assumed the date of 1862 and got the names of the so-called 'first team' a bit wrong.

The players in the famous scarlet and black striped shirts were largely drawn from old boys of Blackheath Proprietary School (1831-1907) which produced many outstanding players - ten internationals and some thirty Oxford or Cambridge 'Blues'.

In those early years of football each club made up its own rules and soon after the Blackheath team was formed the Football Association tried to modify regulations and make the game less violent. Blackheath would have none of this and walked out of a vital meeting because of the proposed rule: 'No player shall carry the ball' (the change that was to produce soccer). They also refused to prohibit holding, pushing, tripping and hacking (deliberate kicking of shins), saying it would 'utterly destroy their game and take away all interest'.

This strong, aggressive team soon had so many supporters that it had to move from the Heath to its own ground, and Blackheath claims to be one of the oldest rugby football sides - if not *the* oldest.

Age may not seem to matter unduly but sport is jealous of priorities. Among erratic captioning of the '1862' photograph, Rhind spotted 'Sir' R.H. Head (but he didn't succeed to his title until twenty-five years later) and there is no record of him playing for Blackheath before 1864. A Blackheath team may well have been formed in 1862 - or even earlier - but it was not necessarily this one, or regularly this size. Numbers then were elastic; here eleven, in a match with Richmond twenty-five. These young Turks make a fine group but it does not establish Blackheath's exact place in the chronology of the game.

165. Playing cricket outside Chesterfield House, 1840.

CRICKET ON THE HEATH

Cricket was first played on Blackheath in the 1820s when the game was spreading like an all-consuming passion throughout the country. The earliest pitches were on the Earl of Dartmouth's estate near Dartmouth Row and opposite St German's Place on the other side of the Heath.

The older team, calling itself the Blackheath Dartmouth Cricket Club, was a gentlemanly semi-aristocratic side which sometimes engaged professionals to win a match on which heavy wagers had been laid. The side was also glad of the services of a headmaster who had moved his school, Alfred House, from Camberwell in 1832 to No. 4 Pond Road. Nicholas Wanostrocht (166) was one of the most unconventional characters in the history of cricket and education.

An incurable cricket enthusiast, Wanostrocht gave all his time to the game and played for Kent, Surrey and England. This may have led to his neglect of his school, which became bankrupt. He tried to recover his fortunes by writing a cricket manual. Under the pseudonym of 'N. Felix, Esq.', his long essay became a classic under the title, *Felix on the Bat*.

The Dartmouth Cricket Club, whose records go back to 1829, flourished until the 1850s when their pitch was ruined overnight. For twenty-five years

166. Nicholas Wanostrocht ('N. Felix Esq.').

167. Watching West Kent Wanderers playing on Blackheath; All Saints is in the background.

the field had been looked after by players and the Dartmouth's groundsmen but was overrun by heavy manoeuvres of the local artillery volunteers from Holly Lodge House. Damage was bad enough for the best Dartmouth club payers to go across the Heath to join the Paragon Cricket Club and the flourishing Montpelier team. The Paragon merged with another local side in 1885 to become the Blackheath Cricket Club at Rectory Field which they shared with the Blackheath Rugby Club.

Cricket became so popular as the century went on that cricketers playing in thirty-six individual games covered every part of the Heath on a Saturday afternoon.

168. The tea interval at a Blackheath cricket match.

Two Blackheath fathers were so keen that they were not satisfied until each had raised ten sons to make up a family side. The landlord of the Hare and Billet started a team in 1856 which fourteen years later became the West Kent Wanderers. They played on the Heath over a period of a hundred years and their particular pitch - to the north of Talbot Place - is still marked on maps as West Kent Field.

An upperclass flavour - symbolized by the casual game with a marquee by the royal residence of Princess Sophia Matilda (165) - changed at the turn of the century when the London County Council took substituted bookings for 'a first-come' setting up of stumps.

After tending their pre-eminent pitch for so many years, the Wanderers considered they had an unchallenged right to the field and it was agreed that they should continue to cut, roll and use this particular part of the Heath for their matches. They continued to play there until the Second World War when they saw stakes driven into their precious pitch for an anti-aircraft detector.

They made a nostalgic return to mark their centenary in 1970 but by then things had radically changed. Clubs of stature had long since acquired private grounds in the Blackheath area where sacred rituals such as the tea interval could be observed (168). On the Heath itself, cricket was simply less popular, with the number of public pitches down from thirty-six to five.

169. Blackheath at Whitsuntide, 1850.

FAIRS ON THE HEATH

When Greenwich Fair was abolished in 1857 the crowds who had enjoyed bank holiday outings for so long walked up the hill and onto Blackheath. They found the showmen and stallholders waiting for them, and even when Blackheath Fair was itself declared illegal eleven years later families continued to visit the Heath in search of entertainment.

A year after the so-called 'total abolition' of Blackheath Fair in 1868 more than 50,000 bank holiday pleasure-seekers failed to recognise the ban. This is typified by one mid-century paterfamilias who has clearly lost all his inhibitions in the refreshment tent (169) and jauntily put on his wife's bonnet. Police half-heartedly patrolling the half-mile between Chesterfield Walk and Maze Hill could not prevent the crowd combining with enterprising showmen to have a good time. The Metropolitan Board of Works went through the motions of keeping law and order by cutting down on the number of licences for stallholders. But even with sideshows halved to fifty, jollities were not markedly subdued.

Around 1900 the attractions of the fair were simple and enduring. Enticing the public's pennies were roundabouts, the Big Wheel, the helter skelter and swings with doubled-seated boats. Blackheath Fair offered all the usual freaks - two-headed animals and a two-headed baby (palpably a clay model), a bearded woman, Tom Thumb and His Wife ('Only 3 ft high'), and there was an eighteen-stone Fat Woman who exhibited huge biceps.

170. The Big Wheel, 1905.

171. Bank holiday funfair c.1900; Shooters Hill Road near the Greenwich Park gate.

Few complained that year after year the side-shows remained the same, that rubber rings never quite settled cleanly over prizes on the wooden blocks; that pennies never rolled down neatly on to winning squares. Such was the fun of the fair.

In the foreground of a photograph of about 1900 (171) are donkeys which could be hired at the entrance of Greenwich Park. Out of fair time they waited for young riders to come along. Tethering rails and a water trough were provided, and for generations of children donkeys were a much loved part of the Blackheath scene. By the turn of the century donkeys, with their noses deep in feeding bags, bore no signs of the cruelties they endured in the past. Let out by gypsies so one report stated, donkeys were... 'stimulated into almost perpetual motion by a ruffian with a bludgeon'. To prevent any such brutalities continuing, four mounted constables were drafted on to the Heath at fair time.

A more congenial recollection of yesterday's fairs comes from a woman who as a girl was always abjured by her mother to stay close to her older brothers and not to spend her fare home. 'You always knew when people had been to the fair', she recalls, 'because you'd see them going home with a little jar with a goldfish in it.'

172. Swings at the fair.

173. The Thames at Greenwich, 1930s.

Along Greenwich Waterfront

The waterfront at Greenwich, stretching a little over two miles from the upward curve of Greenwich Reach to just beyond Deptford Creek, encompasses 500 years of history. A riverside walk passes seventeeth-century buildings and some that are even older, but the main interest focuses on the busy commercial life that developed in the second half of the nineteenth century.

The walk starts at a wharf like this one (A) where the building of iron barges began in the 1850s. Taking a break at the bottom of a slipway are builders and repairers of the huge flat-bottomed barges in the 1930s (173).

A little further south on East Greenwich Marsh is Enderby's Wharf (B). In 1834 three brothers, Charles, Henry and George Enderby, whose private house overlooked the river, started a ropemaking factory. This developed into the manufacture of iron hawsers and then into electric cables. Fed out of the factory like a thread from a spider's web, they were coiled aboard cable ships such as the one here and enabled the *Great Eastern* to make the first successful transatlantic telegraph link with America in 1866.

174. Enderby's Wharf in 1865.

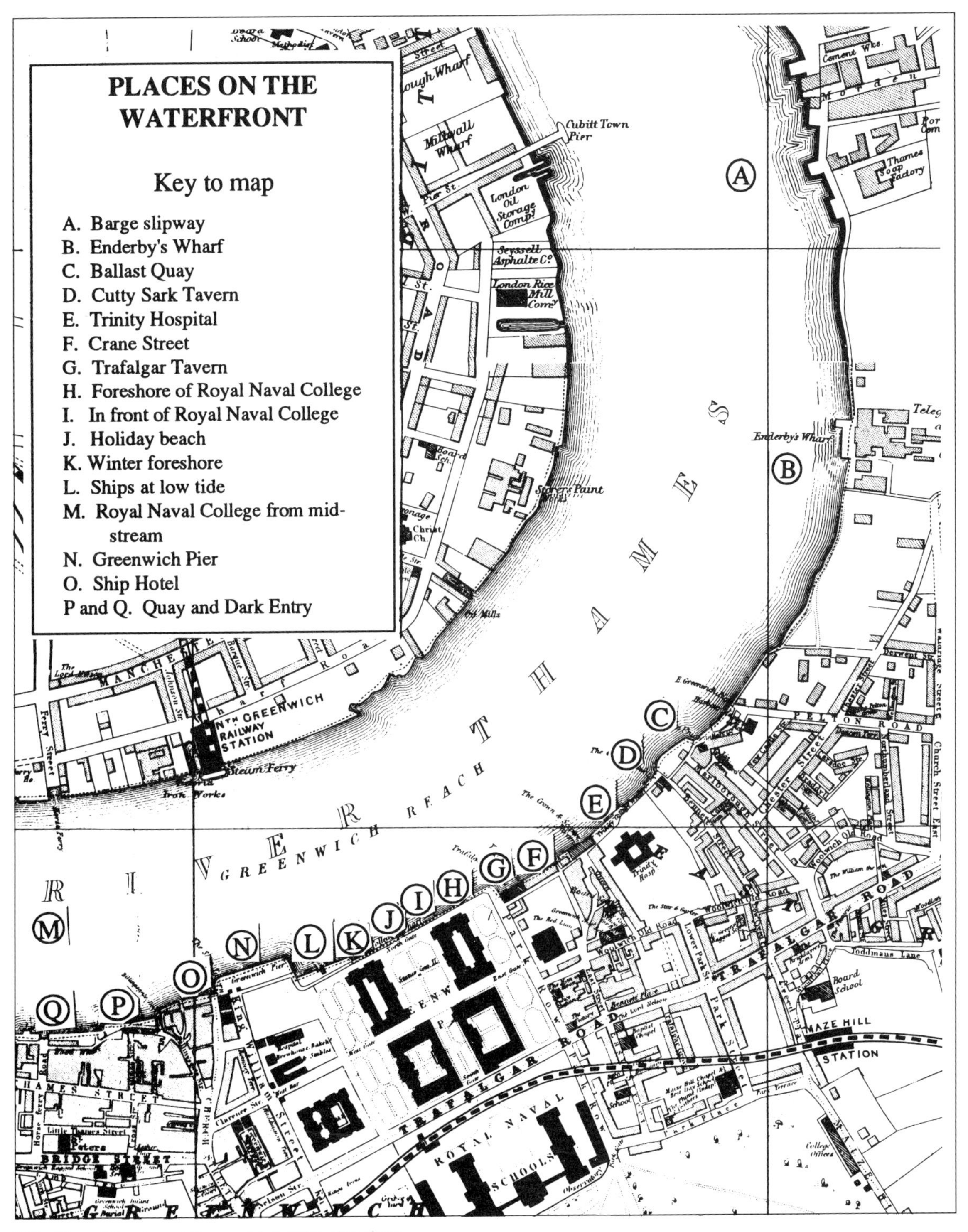

175. Map of the river at Greenwich in Victorian times.

176. Ballast Quay at Greenwich, 1955.

Ballast Quay (C) gained its name from the gravel loaded here. Ships that sailed in with varied cargoes took on loads of gravel brought down Maze Hill from pits excavated on Blackheath and these acted as ballast for the homeward passage. Control of vessels, principally colliers, needed a harbour master's office, and the house, a graceful mid-Victorian building, still exists facing a small private garden overlooking the river. Also on the quayside is a public house, the Cutty Sark (formerly the Union Tavern), with a bowed oriel window (D). The date of this public house is about 1804 but to match its appearance claims a much earlier seventeenth-century origin.

The walk passes under the crane gantries of Greenwich Power Station which was built in 1906 by the LCC to provide electricity for the powered trams that replaced those drawn by horses. Four chimneys tower above Trinity Hospital (E), an almshouse

177. The Cutty Sark public house.

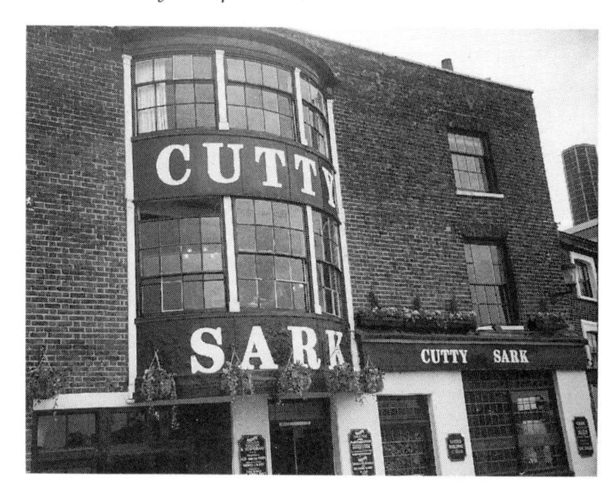

178. Trinity Almshouses.

179. The Three Crowns on the corner of Crane Street and Eastney Street.

founded in 1614, which has a battlemented and stuccoed appearance as a result of rebuilding in 'Gothick' style in 1812.

Administered by the Mercers' Company and with accommodation for twenty-one 'retired Gentlemen of Greenwich', the hospital was founded by Henry Howard, Earl of Northampton. Although he was not originally buried there, the earl kneels in effigy in the small almshouse chapel. His tomb and the little statue arrived nearly a century after his death. The reason for the delay is curious. From boyhood Howard loved Greenwich where he had three houses – Greenwich Castle, Old Court and finally Lumley House by the river. He was forced to leave the Castle by James I (see p. 22), and a lingering resentment decided him to be buried not at Greenwich as he had intended but at Dover Castle. In 1614 he demolished Lumley House and laid the almshouse foundation stone but died the same year. It fell to the Mercers to bring him back to his beloved Greenwich in 1696.

The narrow alleyway beyond the almshouse is called Highbridge. This is said to be the point beyond which by a curious decree of the Venetian Senate in 1453 their ships were not permitted to go up river. The photograph of 1910 shows the extension of the river walk (F) into Crane Street (seen at the junction with of Eastney Street) with the now demolished Three Crowns that overlooked the river.

180. Highbridge.

181. Trafalgar Tavern from Park Row.

In Crane Street, viewed from the opposite direction, there were entrances to several taverns overlooking the river. These included the Yacht (which survives) and the Three Crowns (F, see previous page).

Narrow Crane Street emerges at the bottom of Park Row with the Trafalgar Tavern (G) on the corner. At this date – 1937 – the Trafalgar had ceased to be a tavern and become a centre where unemployed men could have a meal, attend classes and use benches to mend their family's shoes. This was a sad falling off from the time exactly 100 years before when the Trafalgar Tavern had been an interesting feature of Joseph Kay's development of Greenwich. There had been an earlier inn on the site, the George, and it was this small alehouse that the two Kay brothers decided to develop. Discussion went on for five years before the George was demolished and the Trafalgar built largely to Joseph Kay's design. The choice of name was no surprise: by then Greenwich felt the right to bask in Nelson's renown. Working with his brother John and another architect, Kay saw to it that naval associations were kept alive. Rooms were named after Nelson, Hardy, Hawke, Howe, Duncan and Collingwood, and Trafalgar was no idle name; a large riverside room had balconies modelled on the stern galley of *HMS Victory*.

This was one of three taverns that became celebrated for whitebait suppers in the nineteenth century. From being a dish served casually at the many weatherboarded inns along the waterfront, whitebait suppers and public dinners grew into a fashionable Greenwich ritual. The custom seems to have originated when William Pitt, the Younger, and ministerial friends came down river for congenial meals, preludes to more ceremonial later outings. By the 1830s it became a custom for the Prime Minister of the day and most of the Cabinet to make the

182. Trafalgar Tavern.

183. Drawing by Richard Doyle of a whitebait supper at Greenwich in the 1880s.

journey from Whitehall generally just before the House rose for the summer.

A decorated Ordnance barge brought the parties to the various Greenwich taverns. The Trafalgar was chosen by the Liberals; the Tories preferred the Crown and Sceptre and the Ship; Palmerston and Gladstone were among politicians who made the annual pilgrimage.

Something of a mystique surrounded the serving of whitebait which epicures insisted must be lifted fresh from the Thames, cooked within the hour in a copper cauldron over a charcoal fire, and best enjoyed with champagne or punch.

Writers and artists followed the politicians. Dickens was a regular Trafalgar patron and was fêted there by his friends on his return from his first American visit in 1842. 'There is no next morning hangover like that which follows a Greenwich dinner,' he plaintively records.

The popularity of whitebait continued until the end of the century, and the aftermath of the meal is caught by Richard Doyle's drawing in the 1880s (183). It was a scene with which Thackeray, Wilkie Collins, George Cruikshank and Tissot were familiar. But for some reason whitebait lost their popularity in the early years of the next century. When the Trafalgar was restored with a restaurant in 1965, the little fish returned to the menu.

184. *Greenwich Beach in front of the Royal Naval College in summer during the 1930s.*

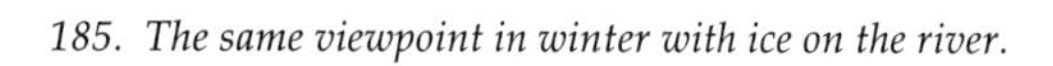

185. *The same viewpoint in winter with ice on the river.*

Between the Trafalgar and Greenwich Pier, the river walk passes in front of the Royal Naval College (H) which lies back out of view in photographs taken at two very different times of year. The foreshore (I) had enough sand and was sufficiently clean and inviting in the 1930s to serve as a holiday beach (J) and, choked with ice, had an Arctic bleakness at an unknown date (K).

The age of sail is evoked by an artist around 1870 who shows ships at low tide (L) and the corner of the old building inscribed 'Carolus II' which is the one surviving part of the palace which King Charles II started but abandoned.

The low water allows a good view of the river steps that have played their part in history. They were used by George I in 1714 when he arrived from Hanover to assume the English Crown, and by the future Queen Caroline on her arrival from Brunswick. Up the steps in the distance Nelson's body was carried for his lying-in-state. By the watergate Francis Chichester was knighted after his voyage round the world in 1967.

The whole range of the Royal Naval College is seen across the water from a pleasure steamer passing up Greenwich Reach in 1934 (M), while to the stern two Thames barges – one of 1882 – work their way down river under sail.

186. Ships beached by the Naval College. Artist unknown.

187. Greenwich Reach looking towards the Royal Naval College, with a Thames spritsail barge in the foreground, 1934.

188. The 1937 panoramic view from the Royal Naval College, left, to the Ship Hotel, right.

In 1937 the Port of London Authority commissioned a photographer to record both sides of the Thames from London Bridge to Greenwich. His superb panorama of docklands showing wharves, piers, factories, riverside pubs and tide-worn landing steps came only just in time. Wartime bombing was to destroy large parts of the waterfront and rebuilding has made some areas hardly recognizable.

189. A paddleboat at Greenwich pier in 1906.

The view of Greenwich in 1937 (N) is much as it would have looked from the time the LCC enlarged the floating pier in 1904. The steamboat arriving two years later (189) is part of a regular service from London Bridge.

The most dramatic change caused by bombing was in the right foreground. Here in 1937 was a building of oppressive grandeur – the Ship Hotel – destroyed by a bomb in 1941 (O). This was the fourth and last in a line of Ship hotels in Greenwich that goes back to early in the seventeenth century. The wartime bomb finally put paid to the Ship that had been built in 1856 and given the full Victorian treatment.

In fact, what stood here (and was destroyed) is only the *facade* of a much bigger earlier hotel. This occurred because the 1856 Ship (with a ballroom, billiard hall and seven private suites for grand occasions) lost its popularity in the 'nineties. As a result the owners auctioned off the contents – they included gas chandeliers from the 1851 Exhibition – and sold the entire back part of the hotel.

On the site of the Ship was built the dry dock into which the *Cutty Sark* clipper was towed in 1954. The surrounding area was cleared and another dry dock found for Sir Francis Chichester's *Gypsy Moth IV* to the right of the domed entrance to the Greenwich Foot Tunnel, built in 1902.

So, although the Ship was still presenting a formidable front to the river in 1937, the hotel by then had a reduced, far less exalted, existence and this came to an end with its Second World War destruction.

190. The sale of the furniture of the Ship Hotel.

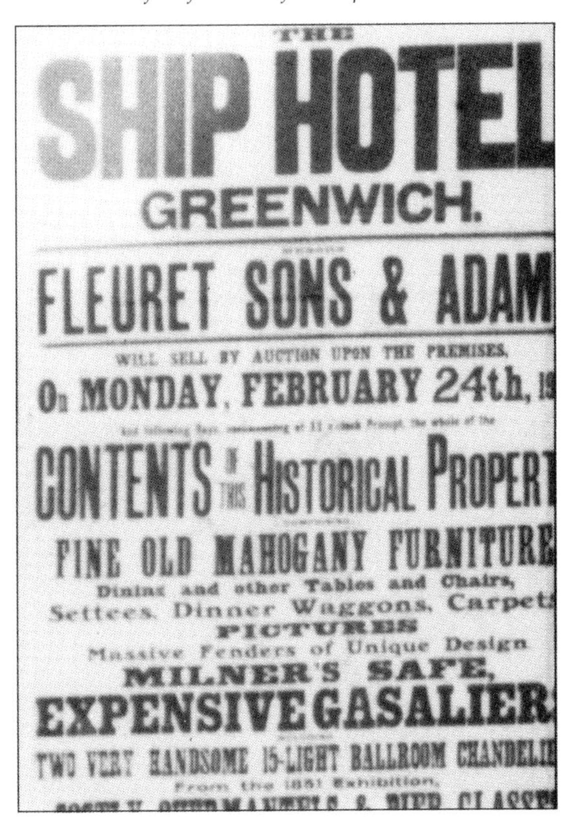

191. The view continuing from tunnel dome past wharves. St Alphege's is in the background, right.

192. Brewhouse Lane (now demolished).

Beyond Garden Stairs and the domed tunnel entrance, riverfront activity and buildings are less clearly defined. The river walk peters out and loses itself in a series of working wharves (today a council housing estate). The main feature of this section is a dark, narrow alleyway known as Brewhouse Lane that ran parallel with the river (192) but was demolished in the 1930s. By the time of this photograph the lane, which ended in ancient Billingsgate Dock, had been demolished and replaced by Dodd's Wharf, occupied by a marine engineering works and a ballast contractor. The view (P and Q), looking east from the appropriately named Dark Entry, offers only the sight of peeling walls, narrow doorways and the sign of a pub called Fuller's Yacht.

In the background is the spire of the Roman Catholic church on Crooms Hill and there is a glimpse of the pedimented west end of St Alphege's. There is then a gap of a quarter of a mile in the panorama before it reaches the estuary entrance to the Ravensbourne river at Deptford Creek (R). The gaunt building on the left is an outbuilding of Phoenix Gas Works, seen in more detail in the 1898 view (193). The *SS Falcon*, lying alongside the repair wharf of the General Steam Navigation Company (S), plies between Greenwich and Scotland. At her stern is the *SS Royal Daffodil*, used by the Port of London Authority for cruises round the docks in 1937. She has a hinged funnel but if she wanted to get three-quarters of a mile up river she would not need to lower it as there

193. Panorama as far as Deptford Creek.

are movable road and rail bridges across the Creek.

Deptford (the alternative name of West Greenwich and just within the borough boundary) is an excuse for going a little inland to see St Nicholas's Church (T). Here in 1593, the Elizabethan dramatist, Christopher Marlowe, killed by a twelvepenny dagger in a mysterious affray at a riverside house, was buried in an unmarked grave.

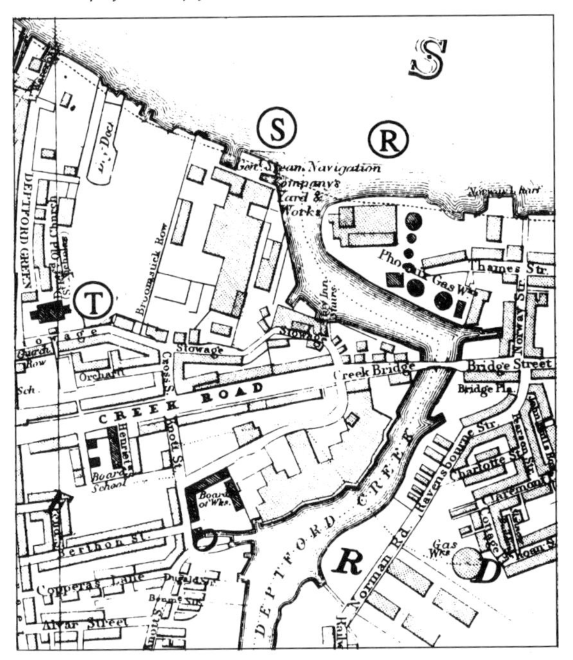

194. Map of the Deptford Creek area.

195. St Nicholas's church.

196. The Turpin Lane entrance to Greenwich Market c1910.

Into the Twentieth Century

RELUCTANT GREENWICH

From the comfortable eminence of Crooms Hill old Greenwich residents moved into the twentieth century with some misgivings. Lately plucked from the County of Kent and now administered by the Metropolitan Borough of Greenwich, they feared loss of individuality and an increase in rates. Half the electorate disdainfully ignored local polls.

On the riverside a huge generating station with belching chimneys was an eyesore justified on the grounds that it was needed to power the new electric trams. The Foot Tunnel, opened in 1902, was a welcome facility for workers going over to Millwall but meant goodbye to a centuries-old ferry. Everyone praised Blackwall Tunnel – then the largest underwater tunnel in the world – but in 1900, three years after its opening, people on the industrial marshes of Greenwich were complaining that workers coming over from Poplar were taking their jobs.

The town's pleasant riverside atmosphere was being lost to industrialism. Picturesque but admittedly far from salubrious dark alleys survived. At one of them – Turpin Lane, the entrance to Greenwich

Market leading from Church Street – stand a group of children (196). Palely looking out from under a pawnbroker's sign, they might pass for Dickensian waifs.

OPTIMISTIC BLACKHEATH

'The Village has a cheerful bustling appearance, while yet retaining just a soupçon of ruralness that appeals so gratefully to the senses', observed *Burrough's Pocket Guide* in 1909. In contrast to Greenwich, Blackheath faced the new century with complacency.

The guidebook describes the Village ('the inhabitants of Blackheath still cling fondly to the title') as healthy, breezy and picturesque. 'Little wonder,' it continues, 'that Blackheath retains its popularity as a residential suburb. It possesses almost every quality...hundreds of houses of all kinds and at rents to suit all incomes; any number of excellent educational establishments; religious and social facilities...a variety of well equipped business premises.'

Offered 'dry and invigorating air', 'a flourishing residential community' and 'rapid and convenient communication with "town" (fifty trains each way from 4 a.m. to past midnight)' those on the look-out for a place to live near London were bound to find Blackheath irresistible.

The desire to please radiates from the advertisements: Reeves and Jones ('for Stylish Millinery'); Henry C. Clark, Job and Riding Master ('Saddle Horses and Quiet Ponies for Children'); Birdseye & Son, Hosier and Hatter ('Specialité – School and Colonial Outfits'); Butcher Curnow and Co. Ltd, Dispensing Chemist ('Hot Water Beds, Air Pillows and Beds for Sale or Hire'); W.J. Lamb, Fruiterer and Florist ('Families waited on Daily for orders'); Ebenezer Smith, Household Removers ('by Rail or by Horse or Motor Traction'); and J. Jobbins, Baker ('Several Varieties of Bread to suit the Particular Palates and Digestion of Customers'), who is clearly in fierce competition with C.A. Rose whose pony and van (197) is at the ready to deliver a 'Free Sample Loaf within a three-mile radius'.

The sound of hands washing in invisible soap is almost audible as the various emporia offer 'special attention', 'honesty in values', 'personal supervision', 'reasonable prices', 'unsurpassable service', 'lowest possible rates' and 'welcome inspection of premises'. Serene new century.

198. Motor buses and taxis quickly replaced horse cabs in the new century but these two drivers - the last in London - were still picking up fares at Blackheath Station in the 1940s.

197. Mr Rose delivering his 'Free Sample Loaf'.

199. Maze Hill in 1900.

MAYHEM ON MAZE HILL

Anyone going to Maze Hill hoping to find splendid examples of the architectural past will be disappointed. Demolition put paid to five impressive Greenwich houses between 1905 and the 1950s. Three were built before the end of the seventeenth century and while this mayhem smacks of vandalism not all of them were masterpieces to start with. As Neil Rhind's research reveals, their fate was more the result of interesting social changes.

The view above (199) is halfway down Maze Hill, one of two main links between Blackheath and Greenwich (the other is Crooms Hill). On the left is a gate into the park. On the right, Maze Hill House is half hidden by many more trees than exist today, but is fully seen from the front (202).

Coming down the hill the first house on the right (with Vanbrugh Castle in the background) was:

MAYFIELD LODGE (200) built in the 1730s. The photograph was taken at the time of the 1906 demolition: No. 119 Maze Hill is now on the site. In 1840 it housed the Maze Hill Establishment, a boarding school for eight young ladies who had to provide a silver fork, knife and spoons and six towels. It was later let for two years to the cricketer Nicholas ('Felix') Wanostrocht (p. 108), and subsequently leased by the Rescue Society for Females (1861-82). It was a ramshackle private house at the time of demolition.

200. Mayfield Lodge.

Next down the hill was
THE GEORGE PUBLIC HOUSE (201), built in 1736. Demolition was about 1905, the approximate date of this photograph, and it was replaced by 117 Maze Hill. It was first leased by Sir Gregory Page to Thomas Wiggins, an East Greenwich carpenter, as a pub. In 1823 John Hartnell used a cottage at the back to print the *Greenwich, Woolwich and Deptford Gazette* (later the *Kentish Mercury.*) It deteriorated with a quick succession of landlords.

201. The George public house.

Then came
MAZE HILL HOUSE (202), built in 1714. It was demolished within forty years of this 1930 photograph and is now developed into an enclave with twenty-seven small houses. It was the retirement home of Admiral Sir John Leake; other tenants included the second Duke of Richmond and a College of Arms Herald. A prosperous family named Collins enlarged the house into a considerable residence with thirteen principal bedrooms, marble hall, Doric portico and weird pedimented attic over the front door. Sold for £2,000 in 1932. Probably Maze Hill's greatest architectural loss.

202. Maze Hill House.

Further down was
CROMBIE HOUSE built in the 1690s. It was demolished in the 1950s after Second World War damage and replaced by 43-45 Maze Hill. The original lease was granted by Sir Gregory Page to a naval captain, (Sir) Charles Malloy. Subsequent tenants included an admiral, a fur broker and the treasurer of the South Eastern Railway Company. The house was run down as early as the First World War.

Last, facing Park Vista, was
DOUGLAS HOUSE built in the 1730s. It was demolished after 1940 following Blitz damage and rebuilt as 23-25 Maze Hill. It was a severe stuccoed building named after Major General Sir John Douglas, who reported Princess Caroline's supposed indiscretions. Other tenants included: an Academy for Young Gentlemen; an office of the South Eastern Railway Company; a girls' school; a working men's club.

Despite these depredations, Maze Hill retains a pair of attractive eighteenth-century houses Nos 111 and 115, and, lower down Nos 47 and 49 which have had distinguished tenants. Restored by the Blackheath Preservation Trust, this last pair retain their imposing 1730 appearance. Although they appear to have been combined – for a while as a boarding school – these were probably designed separately. As he had nine children Stacey Grimaldi, nineteenth-century antiquary and lawyer, may well have needed both. Taken over by the Government during the Second World War and damaged in the Blitz, they have been carefully restored and are back in private hands.

Enemy Attacks

INVASION THREATS

On the direct line of advance from the Continent to London, Blackheath has had to face foreign invasions since Roman and Danish times. Duke Humphrey's Castle and a circle of forts were fifteenth-century defensive precautions, and evidence of threats through history is provided by an extraordinary account which exists of French officers spying out the land in 1707. They described Blackheath as 'a large and beautiful plain where 10,000 men can be placed in order of battle'. No doubt smarting after Blenheim and planning vengeance, the Frenchmen outlined their tactics:

'While our army marches on Shooters Hill and Blackheath, the reserve will make for Woolwich and Greenwich, destroying all the riverside buildings on their way. It is very likely that on this plain the fate of England will be decided. Should a battle take place here the reserve coming up from Greenwich would attack the enemy from the flank...the hill about Deptford and near Greenwich Park is an ideal place to set up our cannons and shoot at the entrenched army.'

NEW-BORN BABY KILLED.

TRAGEDY OF THE RAID ON LONDON OUTSKIRTS.

The Zeppelins made a new record. They not only killed one little child, with its mother and father, in the outskirts of London, they also killed an infant as it was coming into the world, and they killed its mother as well.

The woman lived in one of three adjoining houses which were demolished by bombs. The day before the Zeppelins came she was joyfully looking forward to the birth of her child. It was about a quarter to two in the morning when the booming of guns woke the neighbours. Some of them rose from bed and looked out of the windows. One elderly man, who lives nearly opposite the three ruined houses, was standing at his door when he saw a Zeppelin high overhead.

204. *Three newspaper reminders of the First World War.*

203. *The morning after a Zeppelin raid which struck Tranquil Vale, 14 August 1916.*

ALMSHOUSE SCENES.

"Hole Like a Crater" a Few Yards Away.

The inmates of some almshouses had a marvellous escape. There are almshouses in which old couples live together.

LIVE BOMB.

WAS IT FROM A ZEPP?

GREENWICH FIND.

Workmen engaged at the South Metropolitan Gas Company's works in Thames-street, Greenwich, were cleaning a gas holder to-day when—

They found imbedded in the tar a live explosive bomb.

Early in the war a Zeppelin raid took place at this particular point, and a bomb was reported as having fallen in the neighbourhood without exploding

It was not found.

In modern times the first actual assault on Blackheath came not from the French but the Germans. A Zeppelin dropped a bomb at the top of Tranquil Vale where it joins Camden Row on 14 August 1916 (203). Between 1914 and 1918 there were fifty-seven raids by German planes, and fifty-one by Zeppelins. The airships created a particularly eerie, terrifying effect as they slid silently through moonlit skies. As well as on Blackheath their bombs fell to the north of Shooters Hill, and Greenwich docksides were targets. The total London death roll was 587 and local Greenwich papers made all possible propaganda from the raids (204).

PREPARATIONS 1939

Even before the outbreak of war in September 1939 it was obvious that Blackheath would be on the direct line of German air attack. Even landing by airborne troops was envisaged. Plans were started for air raid shelters round All Saints Church. The Auxiliary Fire Service converted the Prince of Wales Pond into a reservoir on which it could draw to deal with incendiary bombs. Searchlight batteries, anti-aircraft and Bofors gun emplacements were set up on the Heath.

Barrage balloons were particularly reassuring. They, at least, would keep enemy planes at a height. They were tethered on the Kidbrooke side of the Heath and in the gravel pits opposite Vanbrugh Terrace where, when they were not flying, they could be kept inflated and to some extent protected below ground level.

Organized games on the Heath stopped and gave way to trenches to prevent the landing of enemy planes, parachutists and troops in gliders. Everyone became security conscious and cameras have left only very vague records of the mounds that dotted the grass to foil invaders. When the expected air attack did not come many of the trenches were filled in. Too many people were falling into them during the blackout.

205. A trench dug near All Saints Church, 1939.

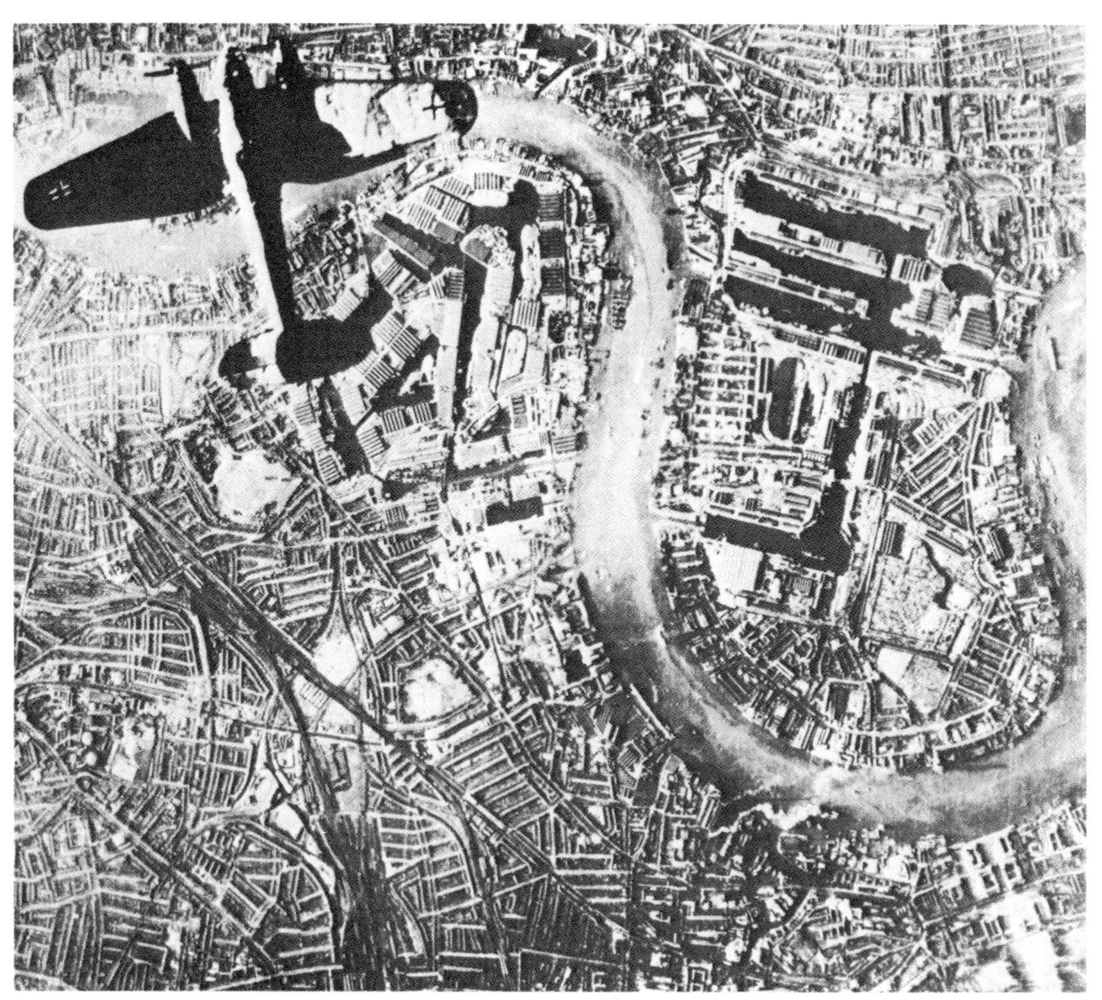

206. A German Heinkel plane over Greenwich in September 1940.

THE START – SEPTEMBER 1940

After a year of the 'phoney war' the Germans made their first mass attack with 400 planes around teatime on 7 September 1940. The vulnerability of Greenwich is clear from the photograph above (206) of a Heinkel 111 on that first day. If Luftwaffe crews had time to take each other's photographs it suggests that they were not facing enough flak.

Two nights earlier the enemy had dropped incendiaries causing eighteen fires in East Greenwich. Attacks continued for fifty-seven nights without let up. Effective defence was impossible.

The first recorded deaths in Blackheath came six days after the start of the Blitz when a bomb landed on the rural outskirts – Wricklemarsh Road, Kidbrooke. Five people were killed. They appear to have been part of a family named Edmonds. The next civilians to become victims of the bombing were the Davies family in Shooters Hill Road.

The comfortable belief that death does not strike twice in the same place was confounded by two attacks on the Invicta Road School near the Old Dover Road. A 110 lb bomb crashed through the roof of the school – acting as an auxiliary fire station –without exploding and two firemen bravely carried it into the playground. Two months later – the same night as the Coventry raid – a parachute bomb fell on the school. Among the twelve firemen killed was Arthur Grant who two days earlier had received the George Medal for his previous gallantry.

Destruction and fatalities during the winter of 1940-41 make depressing reading. They included Greenwich Observatory (207), the Maritime Museum, Greenwich Hospital, the Paragon (two killed),

207. The Royal Observatory bombed.

St Alphege's (completely gutted), the Ursuline Convent, Crooms Hill, Sieman's factory in Grotes Place.

Nightly horror ended for a while on 10 May 1941 but on that particular night the fatality roll was heavy – a family of four killed on Shooters Hill; 250 yards of Trafalgar Road and tram rail rippd up by six half-ton bombs (ten killed); Greenwich Baths blown up (a warden killed nearby); a police inspector fatally injured in East Greenwich. South-east London then took a breath after the killing of 1,436 people, of which 130 were children.

The respite lasted until 1944 when at 2.05 on the morning of 23 June a strange plane-like missile with wings and a flaming tail came through thick clouds, cut out and landed on a searchlight battery on the Heath (five killed, six injured). Another V1 at 8 a.m. made a direct hit on the balloon barrage headquarters in Beaconsfield Road, Westcombe Park (two killed, twenty-one injured).

In the doodle-bug assault lasting eleven weeks (during which the Second Front started) at least forty-nine landed in the area. A particularly grim incident in Greenwich Church Street occurred after a direct hit on a mansion block (from which thirteen bodies were brought out after a large rescue operation). Another was on Lewisham Hill when twenty properties were destroyed (thirteen lives lost). Greenwich Park Railway, brought back to use by the war took a direct hit (209).

A map based on Civil Defence records in 1944 (210) shows the buzz-bomb landings that ended on 1 September when the launching sites were overrun by the Allies. One V2 rocket on Blackheath the following year is also shown.

208. The back of two bombed houses in the Paragon.

THE PARAGON DECIMATED

Hitler's notorious 'Baedeker raids' might almost have had the Paragon on their agenda. There was progressive destruction of the Georgian crescent. Nearby buildings in Georgian style – Bryan House, Colonnade House, Paragon House and others in South Row – were badly damaged in 1940, two irreparably. In March the following year No. 10 the Paragon was completely destroyed by a direct hit; and No. 9 adjoining was burnt out.

To overlook the Heath had disadvantages. Guns and balloons might seems a protection but anti-aircraft fire brought down V1 rockets uncomfortably close and they exploded on impact. This is how Nos 1 and 2 in the Paragon crescent suffered so severely in 1944 (208). Where the big bombs missed, incendiaries, shell splinters and anti-personnel bombs added to the dereliction. The Paragon catastrophies had only one compensation. When rebuilding took place after the war, C. Bernard Brown, an architect of dedication and sensibility, carried out restoration with great care. He even improved on what had been there because he removed some extensions and additions which had marred the Paragon's pre-war appearance.

209. Clearing away debris from Greenwick Park Railway.

210. The intensity of the VI attacks can be judged from the number of landings in the Greenwich-Blackheath area in the eleven weeks from the middle of June 1944 to 1 September when the enemy launching sites were over-run. Of the V2 rocket landings only the one on Blackheath village (8 March 1945) is marked (X). The map is not of the same date as the raids.

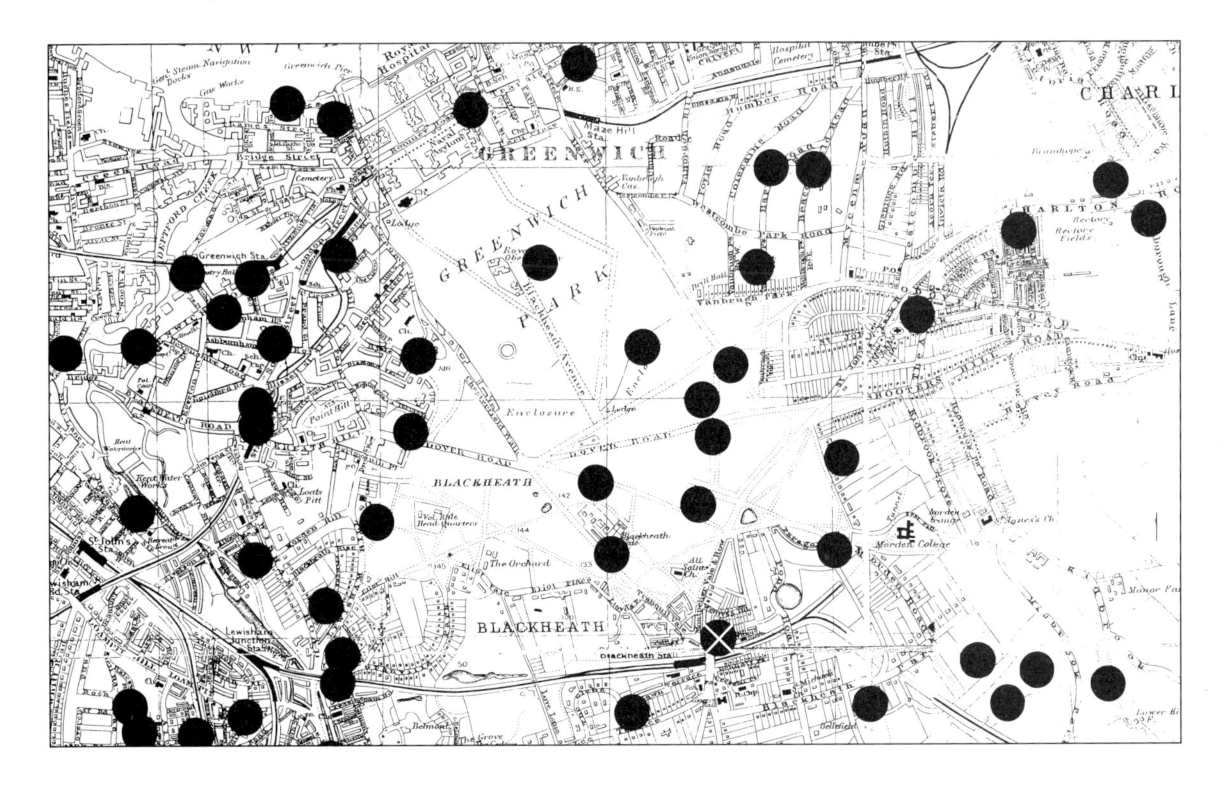

211. Bombing next to Montpelier Vale. All Saints Church and the Heath in the background.

FINAL BLACKHEATH BOMBING

Blackheath suffered one final and devastating blow. It took place on 8 March 1945 – a date when seemingly it should never have happened because news was coming through that the Germans were evacuating the launching pads at Peenemunde. The war had only eight weeks to go.

A schoolboy recalls the day. As he told the story to Lewis Blake (an invaluable recorder of wartime in south-east London), he was sitting an English exam and facing an essay topic 'An evening spent at home'. Derisively he was wondering if this meant in an air raid shelter when a great explosion came from some way off. He simply carried on. In those days rockets were so common that everyone had become fatalistic. As he was finishing his paper there came another explosion. 'A mighty crack seemed to arch over the heaven or rend them apart' is how he described the noise that shook floors and windows. 'It was incredible to think that the crash emanated from Blackheath Village nearly two miles away.'

The time was six minutes past midday. As with all V2s there was no warning – just a tearing sound 'like an express train' as the rocket landed vertically from a height of fifty miles and faster than the speed of sound. It was a direct hit on the Methodist Church just south of Wemyss Road (site of the present day car park) and demolished buildings in Blackheath Grove.

The Post Office, the Express Dairy plant and shops in Montpelier Vale were severely damaged. It was said that every window in 140 shops was shattered. With calm understatement, Blackheath High School announced in the local guide two days later that plans for reopening the junior school would be 'unavoidably delayed'.

The number of people injured and carried from the debris was 134 but by a miracle – if it can be called that – only five people were killed.

212. Aerial view of the Heath showing wartime scars.

AFTERMATH

While the war was being fought devastation was inevitable and had to be endured, but subsequent drabness was difficult to accept. Hardly a house in Blackheath had escaped damage of some sort. People who had been evacuated and those returning from the Services set to work to renovate their homes but for several years the Heath itself remained a sad mess.

A view looking south-west (212) shows ghostly reminders of what had suffered and needed restoration. On the grass are the marks left after removal of guns, searchlights and huts where the army had lived for five wartime years. Squatters took over some of the rusting Nissen huts and for a while there was a LCC plan which never materialized to house the homeless in two rows of pre-fabs opposite St German's Place (in the foreground).

When food was short no one objected to the acre or two of allotments that had been encouraged opposite Eliot Place. When Ministry of Information posters were exhorting rosy-faced girls to 'Dig for Victory' they had seemed splendidly patriotic, but owners of surrounding houses looked out at rotting cabbages with increasing distaste.

And what, people asked, was to be the future of Holly Hedge Bungalows? This was a colony of eighty pre-fabs (distantly visible in the aerial view), which had been laid out with roads and little gardens alongside Mounts Pond Road. They had been gratefully occupied by bombed-out families from Greenwich, but in 1947 hardly matched the old dignity of the Dartmouth Estate. There was much wailing from the revived Blackheath Society and signing of protests by people who were severely reminded by the authorities that sacrifices must be expected to solve the housing shortage.

Slowly the thousands of blown-out and boarded windows were repaired and fastidious preservationists studied an article by the Georgian Group on the scale and design of glazing bars and how they were to be preferred to single sheets of Victorian plate glass.

Eventually the Eliot Place allotments disappeared and the Holly Hedge Bungalows became a forgotten nightmare. Instead, with 10,000 local people waiting for homes, four acres of land by Pond Road near the Paragon were acquired for council flats and in the 1950s an even larger LCC estate of 289 flats and houses appeared on the fringes of the Cator Estate.

Bomb rubble was tipped into old gravel pits such as Washerwomen's Bottom opposite Royal Parade and the ground levelled and grassed. The Heath was ready to receive back its sportsmen.

Post-War Blackheath

THE GREAT SPAN BATTLE

Hardly had Blackheath put its war-battered houses in order than the village was faced with a new threat to tranquillity. The Cator Estate, long admired for the Georgian flavour of its houses, was invaded by Span Developments. Established residents sipping Sunday morning drinks in their 1820s pastel-coloured villas in such places as Pond Road (213) were caught almost unawares by the new menace. Who was this man Eric Lyons, and what devastation was he threatening to their green and pleasant sanctuary?

The invasion came from Surrey where Lyons, a radical architect, had already brought Span houses to Richmond and Twickenham. A dynamic disciple of Maxwell Fry and Walter Gropius, he had infiltrated Blackheath with the help of a Fifth Columnist, a Blackheath builder, Leslie Bilsby.

The first battlefield for the Lyons-Bilsby attack was four acres south of Priory Lane where they proposed to demolish the houses to build sixty-one modern flats. This was in 1956, and the following year Span bought three acres off Foxes Dale to build a further forty-four flats.

The Span proposals were simple and seemingly admirable – to provide young and medium-income house buyers who had modern tastes with small open-plan houses at around £3,450 for a 99-year lease. It was a progressive conception and if they had objections old guard Blackheath residents found them weakened because Span houses were thoughtfully, aesthetically planned.

With terraces on different levels, garden courts and trees to be seen through large windows, they had considerable appeal. Even if some of them were box-like and uniform, the charm of a prototype three-storey house in Foxes Dale was undeniable. With paved garden and sun balcony screened with glass and with a pergola, it only needed Riviera weather.

213. Pond Road.

214. A 1959 Span house with a South of France look.

215. Group of Span houses. Different levels and hung-tile walls dispelled monotony.

Newspaper headlines (216) reflected the opposition felt when Span's demolition and construction reached the very citadel of conservation – Blackheath Park – in 1958 and down came a Regency house to create Hallgate with twenty-six flats on two levels. Over the next few years Span was accused of surreptitiously buying up old property and at public inquiries there were demands that 'flat-faced' houses should not spoil the area.

Two particular buildings under threat symoblized the battles of new versus old. The Priory, a Regency folly with an eccentric church-style tower, had only a romantic claim for preservation. Span bought the two acres on which it stood and Lyons turned a stumbling block to his advantage by incorporating the tower into his development. For better or worse it became more of a folly than before.

Far more controversial was the Hall. On six acres between Foxes Dale and Brooklands Park, it had a preservation order and for ten years stood empty while ideas for its future were aired. But Span would not compromise. They said it was absurd to preserve an old building for its own sake when they could replace it with something socially and architecturally better. Span won. By 1963 deterioration was so great that the 1806 mansion came down to be replaced by a yellow brick building with angular towers, irregular windows and obtruding sentry-box entries.

With time, Span houses became more acceptable even to their fiercest critics, and statistics suggest that Span's philosophy has been justified. Over a period of eleven years eight houses of the Regency period were demolished. In comparison 240 Span houses and 181 Span flats have been built. In all, Span has been responsible for changing the face of thirty acres of Blackheath and putting up 487 dwellings. Few would now quarrel with Nikolaus Pevsner's approval of Span's "careful landscaping, ingenious layouts and 'friendly' detailing".

Property Problems

Clash at Blackheath

£10,000 HOUSES ARE 'COARSE'

By HAROLD BRETT

DEVELOPMENT PLAN FOR BLACKHEATH

MAINTAINING "SPECIAL CHARACTER OF AREA"

FIRM 'BUYIN UP PROPERT

RESIDENTS OBJEC TO DEVELOPMENT

MR. LESLIE BILSBY, joint managing director of Span Developments, was accused of surreptitiously buying up property in an attempt to infiltrate into the area, when a Ministry of Housing and Local

No action on Span plan complaint

a Staff Reporter

HOUSING PLANS APPROVED

BLACKHEATH AREA DEVELOPMENTS

DECISION BY MR. BROOKE QUERIED

BLACKHEATH CASE FOR TRIBUNALS COUNCIL

216. Newspaper cuttings describing the Span controversy.

Millennium Greenwich

The first indication that Greenwich might play a major role in Britain's millennium festivities came in a telephone call to the National Maritime Museum in 1993. The idea of a national celebration had been floated as early as 1984 when an enterprising businessman announced plans for a great exhibition in 2001 to a packed reception for leaders of industry at the House of Commons. Not only would this extravaganza herald in the brave new year of 2001 but it would also commemorate the 150th anniversary of the Great Exhibition in Hyde Park. Exactly where in London the extravaganza would take place was left vaguely in the air.

Little more was heard of this ambitious enterprise but the seeds had been sown. Nine years later, when the director of development at the National Maritime Museum took a call from the United States, Greenwich realized it held a trump card. An American television company wished to hire one of the museum's buildings – the old Royal Observatory – for 'millennium night', which public consensus had resolutely decided to celebrate on 31 December 1999. The lure was the imaginary meridian line – longitude zero – which passes across the Observatory courtyard. The International Meridian Treaty signed in Washington D.C. in 1884 had established in law that every new day starts at mean midnight at the cross-hairs of the Airy Transit Circle telescope at the Royal Observatory. Greenwich is the place where time begins.

218. Decontamination work in progress on the site of the Dome. A hole had to be left in the Dome's roof for the Blackwall Tunnel ventilation shaft.

217. The Greenwich Marsh from Canary Wharf.

There were, however, contenders in other parts of Britain and after much see-sawing indecision Greenwich's bid to host the country's principal celebration was finally given the go-ahead in June 1997. It has proved to be the catalyst for the regeneration of the waterfront.

A thousand acres of derelict land on the river's edge had recently been identified as ripe for transformation. Investors had begun to recognize the potential and news of the year-long millennium festivities precipitated a rush from drawing boards.

The festival would be held on wasteland crossed by the meridian line downriver from the town, on land once known as the Greenwich Marsh and now upgraded to the more gentrified name of the Greenwich Peninsula (217). Decontamination of a disused gasworks on the site was almost complete. Construction of the extension of the Jubilee line was underway and the North Greenwich station interchange was well advanced. Work had also started on the twin tunnels being cut beneath the Thames to carry the computer-operated Docklands Light Railway from the Isle of Dogs to a new station beside the *Cutty Sark*. And design proposals unveiled the previous summer by Mike Davies of the Richard Rogers Partnership and Gary Withers of Imagination for a huge translucent dome supported by masts had been approved. Contracts were quickly signed and workers were immediately able to sink the first of 8,000 concrete piles. The £758 million project became a visible reality when the 20-acre roof – the largest in the world – covering the Dome's exhibition space was finished precisely twelve months later.

There were other changes, too. On the Peninsula, south of the Dome, construction of more than 3,000 homes overlooking a new fifty-acre parkland began and shops, a school and an hotel on the outer boundaries started to go up. A further 550 houses were built on desolate land to the west of Deptford Creek (194) and a cruise liner terminal in Greenwich Reach with restaurants, shops and entertainment facilities will revitalise a dismal stretch of land east of the Creek. The new pier and a new-look Cutty Sark Gardens will give a more welcoming face to visitors arriving by boat.

ROYAL NAVAL COLLEGE MOVES OUT

Greenwich's naval connections, begun when Henry VIII created dockyards at Woolwich and Deptford, ceased after almost five centuries when the Royal Naval College, which had occupied Wren's baroque buildings for 175 years, moved out in 1998, and a 150-year lease was granted to the University of Greenwich. Links with the sea, however, remain and the expansion of the National Maritime Museum – with sixteen new galleries in the Neptune

219.The Dome on the Greenwich Peninsula.

220. Royal Naval officers at the Watergate waiting to salute a passing naval vessel, a custom which ceased in 1998.

Picture courtesy of NMEC/QA Photos

Court – reaffirms the riverside town's strong historical associations with the sea.

A final accolade has been the recognition of Greenwich as an area of 'outstanding universal value'. Its dramatic landscape and rich architectural heritage were designated a World Heritage Site by UNESCO in December 1997, the fifteenth in the United Kingdom to be placed on the international list. With the arrival of the millennium, living history continues to run through Greenwich.

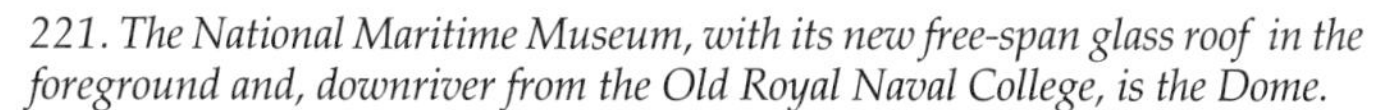

221. The National Maritime Museum, with its new free-span glass roof in the foreground and, downriver from the Old Royal Naval College, is the Dome.

INDEX

Illustrations are indicated by an asterisk.